FL MESEN. PECZORA FL
AVREA ANVS
YSSA
YSSA FL
IVHRA
INDE VNGARORV ORIGO
ARE
CIALE
PINEGA
CIRCO
KVLVYO
MESEN
COLMOGOR
SLATA BABA
OBEACAS
INA PRO VI NCIA
ARTANICZA
FL SOSSA
FL SILVT
CINGVLVS TER
VSTINGO
FL PINEGA
PECZORA FL
TEROM
TVMEN
PERMIA PROVINCIA
FL VISTORQIA
PERMIA
FL IVG
KITHAY
LACVS
FL VIACKHA
KASTROMA
VOLGA
CZEREMISSA POPVLI
ORLOW
CHOTELNICZ
MERIA
SLOVODA
FL RECZICZA
MVROM
OCCA
BASILOWGOROD
CASAN
CA SIMOW GOROD
NOVOGARDIA INFERIOR
FL SVRA
FL VIAGLA
MORDVA POPVLI
ORIENS
HENCE TANAIS
FL VIECZNA
9 18 27 36 45 54 63 72 81 90
DISTANTIA PER MILIARIA
TANAIS FONTES
RHA GRECÆ
FL WOLGA RVTHENICE
EDEL TARTARICE
ZAICK FL
WELIKIPREVOS. SEV TRAIECTVS MAGNVS
SIBIER PROVINCIA
NAGAVSKI TARTARE
TARTARIA
CIRCASI PETIGOISKY
CIRCASI POPVLI
ASTRACHAN
SORAYCZIK
SCHAMACHI
MARE CASPIVM

DESCRIPTION OF MOSCOW AND MUSCOVY

Portrait of the author by an unknown artist

DESCRIPTION OF MOSCOW AND MUSCOVY

1557

Sigmund von Herberstein

EDITED BY
BERTOLD PICARD

TRANSLATED BY
J. B. C. GRUNDY

LONDON
J. M. DENT & SONS LTD

Published in Austria in 1966 under the title of
Beschreibung Moskaus der Hauptstadt in Russland samt des Moskowitischen Gebietes by Verlag Styria

Made in Great Britain
at the
Aldine Press · Letchworth · Herts
for
J. M. DENT & SONS LTD
Aldine House · Bedford Street · London
First published in this edition 1969

SBN: 460 07687 6

CONTENTS

ILLUSTRATIONS

NOTE ON THE ILLUSTRATIONS

The line illustrations, and the coloured portrait of the author in robes presented to him by the ruler of Muscovy, are here reproduced—we believe for the first time in England—by courtesy of the British Museum; the frontispiece from an original water-colour bound into an extra-illustrated volume; the maps and figures from engravings in early printed editions (none later than 1551) of Herberstein's *Description* and of his other autobiographical work about his general career in the Imperial diplomatic service.

EDITOR'S PREFACE

In 1549, in the interval between the Smalkaldic League and the Peace of Augsburg, Freiherr Sigmund von Herberstein's book on Russia was published in Vienna by Aegidius Adler and Hans Kohl. *Rerum Moscoviticarum Comentarii* was the title of this work written in humanistic Latin, and it rapidly enjoyed a considerable success. Two years later a new edition was required, edited by the Viennese doctor and historian Wolfgang Lazius and issued in Basle by the still existent *Offizin*, or printing-office, of the celebrated Oporinus, which also published the third edition in 1556. Only a year later, Michael Zimmermann published in Vienna the author's own version in German: 'Moscovia, the chief town of Russia, . . . together with the Muscovite territory and a description of its borders. . . .' The maps and illustrations, drawn by Augustin Hirschvogel, Hans Sebald Lautensack and others, were more numerous than in the earlier editions and offered glimpses of remote Russia with its broad rivers and vast forests, the Kremlin set amid the wooden houses of the town, the mighty grand-duke and martial horsemen, muffled travellers huddling in their sleighs and accompanied by men on skis through the snow-wrapped landscape and even of some of the greater moments of the author's own life, such as his knighting by the hand of Emperor Maximilian I. It was not Herberstein's own translation which found favour with the public but the German version issued in 1563 by the Basle historian and doctor Heinrich Pantaleon in his native town. In 1567 there was a further edition and also one in Prague; in 1576, 1579 and 1589 came those of Frankfurt, and in 1795 that of St Petersburg upon the instructions of Catherine the Great. To date the last German versions have been those brought out in Erlangen by Wolfram von den Steinen in 1926 and the selection issued in Graz and Vienna in 1963 by Reinhard Federmann under the title of *Priests and Boyars*.

The success of the edition in Latin was even greater. After the two Basle editions already mentioned there were further ones in Antwerp in 1557, Frankfurt in 1560, in Basle again in 1567, 1571, 1573 and 1574, in Frankfurt in 1600, and in 1841 in Berlin and St Petersburg. Of the translations into languages other than German there are two in Italian, one as early as 1550 and one in 1583, both from Venice; there are also two in English, published in London in 1576 and 1582, a Czech one published in 1786 in Prague, three Russian versions, which appeared in 1847, 1866 and 1908 in St Petersburg, and one Slovenian issued in 1951 in Ljubljana (Laibach).

But reference to the wide distribution and large number of editions —in the four decades between 1549 and 1589 there were eighteen of them, all told—is not needed as indirect testimony of the success and fame of Herberstein's book. There is express contemporary evidence of it, such as that of Henricus Glareanus, an historian teaching in Freiburg im Breisgau, who declared that no book had filled him with such profound admiration for many years nor given him greater profit, and that all friends of geography must esteem it highly.[1] Or the words of Daniel Mauch, cathedral archivist in Worms and erstwhile secretary of a papal mission to Moscow at the time of Herberstein's second Russian embassy, who wrote: 'Let every cultivated man be glad to pay twenty paltry gulden for this book, which will gladden him more than gold and precious stones.'[2] And if we make some slight allowance for the motive of publicity there is honourable praise in the prefatory dedication to Pantaleon's translation of 1563, in which he writes that Herberstein 'is not one of those wanton people who portray something merely to give pleasure or from hearsay but a lofty, intelligent and meritorious man of good family who was dispatched on several occasions, on behalf of His Majesty the Holy Roman Emperor, as envoy to the Grand-duke of Moscow, whose domains he surveyed, informing himself industriously of all their business . . . How diligently he describes to us the names and usages of the Russians! Who else could present to us so precisely the religion, customs and military affairs of the Russians? How soundly he describes, in proper geographical manner, the entire territory of the Muscovites and all the adjacent frontiers and peoples, tracing the roads from the German lands to Poland, Lithuania, Moscow, nay even to the Tatars and the neighbouring regions, to which few have so far penetrated! All this he does with a rare modesty, correcting with forbearance the errors of the scribblers who had previously written of these parts. In this way he notes everything with such order that the reader thinks

[1] Reprinted in Johannes Dantiscus, *Soteria*, Vienna 1560 (J 3r).

[2] Written to Herberstein from Worms, 20 March 1560 (MSS Collection of Austrian National Library, Vienna, cod. 13598, 323r).

to travel with him into this country, inspecting the Grand-ducal court and then returning home to Germany.'[1]

Herberstein's success, as is also clear from the above quotation, arose first and foremost from the novelty of what he was describing. For many centuries people in the Holy Roman Empire and elsewhere in Europe had known little of Russia. Interest in the Slavonic nations had been almost wholly absorbed by the immediate neighbours to the east, the Wends, the Poles, the Hungarians. On the other hand the White Russians, Ukrainians and Great Russians, whose principalities and trading republics—with the Grand-duchy of Kiev at their head—had been in existence since the ninth century, lay too far removed from the European observer. There were official contacts of course, but the effect of these embassies and alliances remained superficial; even historically and geographically, their brief accounts of Russia often read like a fairy-tale. In the thirteenth century, it is true, the influence of the German Order of Knights and of the Hanseatic League began to be felt: in Livonia the Order's territory bordered on Russian ground and its copious archives provide much information about the Russian neighbours. Nor are the commercial agreements, chronicles and correspondence of the Hansa, which pushed its depots far forward to the east, any more informative about them. But just as the Empire paid scant attention to the eastern policy of the Order or the Hansa, so it gave little heed to their reports about Russia. Thus central and western Europe heard scarcely anything about the submergence of most of the Russian states in the thirteenth century by the Tatars and of the rise of the Grand-duchy of Moscow, whose rulers were striving to gather all the Russian territories together and free themselves from Mongolian dominance. When towards the end of the fifteenth century they succeeded, the rest of the world discovered with astonishment this new great power behind the screen of Poland and Lithuania and sought to incorporate it into its policies. A lively diplomatic traffic developed and the Empire often found itself in alliance with Muscovy; in religious affairs there was a series of attempts at union, starting at Rome. Because of all this it became desirable and necessary to learn more about this exotic and suddenly important country in the east, and Ivan the Terrible's sudden attack upon Livonia soon after the middle of the sixteenth century made the matter more urgent.

There was little to satisfy this need—or even to serve Herberstein in the preparation of his book. There were printed reports of the

[1] *Moscouiter wunderbare Historien*, Basle 1563 (*2v, *3r).

travels of Venetian envoys, such as Ambrosius Contarini's of 1487, based upon personal experience but providing no general picture. Other authors used as their main sources conversations with Russians living in Europe, perhaps as ambassadors. Such was the case with Paolo Giovolo [1] of Rome and with the Catholic theologian, subsequently Bishop of Vienna, Johann Fabri, whose book appeared like Giovolo's in 1525 and had the unusual feature of a survey of religious conditions in Russia. On the other hand Sebastian Münster attempted a wider conspectus in his *Cosmographia universa* of 1541, but his sources were exclusively the writings of others. All these works are overshadowed by the *Tractatus de duabus Sarmatiis* of the Cracow prebendary and doctor Mathias Miechowski which appeared in 1517 and, a year later, in a German translation by Luther's opponent Dr Johann Eck, but which had curiously little effect and was soon forgotten.

Herberstein was the first to fill this ever more apparent gap. But it was not only the circumstances of his journeys or the fewness and slightness of competing accounts which brought his *Moscovia* to such fame and made of him the discoverer of Russia. His book retained its status in later times despite the appearance of other relevant works, of which however the more significant, such as those of Guagnini and Hosius in the sixteenth century, depended most upon their forerunner. His ability to fashion European posterity's image of Russia for several centuries sprang largely from the breadth and accuracy of his accounts of eastern Europe, a merit accorded special praise in the words quoted from Pantaleon above. It is a truly comprehensive work, not confined to Russia but treating of that country's situation amid its neighbours and thereby involving them also. Thus Herberstein becomes expansive about the Tatars, dealing with their history, their mode of life, and describing the characteristic aspects of their politics and landscape.[2] He deals similarly with the Lithuanians and the coastal countries of the Baltic, including the whole of Scandinavia. But the main target remains the portrayal of Russia which, apart from the section dealing with the experiences of foreign diplomats in Moscow, forms a compact theme underlying the geographical ramifications to the north, south and east. Throughout Herberstein adds to the text his private signals, his own love of history causing him to give to the survey of the history of the Grand-duchy of Moscow and of Russia

[1] The sixteenth-century historian.

[2] The reader is reminded that the present text is a selection from the longer original.

an especially broad treatment, and similarly to the Russian Orthodox faith, to which his own master, King Ferdinand I, was particularly well disposed. Again from personal interest he accords especial attention to the facts of geography and, remarkable in a diplomatist, to the reception of foreign envoys. Between these larger chapters Herberstein devotes himself in briefer but no less accurate or suggestive passages to other topics, to government and administration, the army and the course of justice, social conditions, trade and commerce and daily life.

The breadth and thoroughness of his accounts were made possible

Maximilian I and Ferdinand I

by the mass of the material he had collected. He was not dependent upon the few existing works of writers from central or western Europe and when he turned to written sources they had to be first-hand—the annals of monasteries, city-states (such as Novgorod) and principalities, constitutional regulations, state laws, ecclesiastical resolutions, records of travel. Such manuscript documents were not to be lighted upon in western Europe, of course: they had to be tracked down in Russia, and Herberstein found the opportunity for this in 1517–18 and 1526–7 when two diplomatic missions took him to the court of the Grand-duke Basilius III. His first mission, on behalf of Emperor Maximilian I, was designed to bring about a settlement between the hostile Poles and Russians and thus prepare the way for a common movement of all Christian states against the Turks, on behalf especially of hard-pressed Hungary. Herberstein came home empty-handed, but eight years later he set off again upon the same errand, this time as ambassador of King Ferdinand I and in the company of the Spanish Count

Nogarola, sent by Emperor Charles V. Peace between the warring neighbours could still not be established by the Habsburg envoys, but after long and tedious negotiations with the Muscovite counsellors and the representatives of Poland and Lithuania, and supported by a papal nuncio, they at least achieved a five-year armistice. For Hungary this came too late; shortly before the settlement this country had suffered decisive defeat by the Turks at Mohacs. Amid the negotiations in Moscow Herberstein now found time to look about him. He procured the documents already mentioned and widened his knowledge by talking to the Russians and to foreigners who had been in Russia for some time. Each one of these informants who seemed to him experienced and reliable he peppered with questions, whether they were his diplomatic colleagues, interpreters engaged in the negotiations, the quartermaster or other members of the official Russian escort, officials of the government and administration, the confidant and treasurer of the Grand-duke, members of the princely nobility, the squireage or the common people. To what Herberstein read and heard was added what he found out for himself. Counting both his missions together he stayed ten months in Moscow and one in Mozhaisk, not far away. His outward and return journeys in Russia lasted many weeks, usually taking him with minor variations from Lithuania to Moscow via Smolensk and back by the same route, though once he went farther north by Polotsk, Novgorod and Tver (now Kalinin). What Herberstein describes, from the Grand-duke and his officials to Church affairs or the life of the common people, he had seen mostly with his own eyes; many of the landscapes and settlements he knew from personal experience, for he was familiar with the Russians from thousands of encounters.

Nevertheless it was not easy to come by documents or witnesses and find out for himself about conditions in Russia. The Grand-duke, it is true, allowed the Habsburg envoys on several occasions to take part in Orthodox worship and he invited them to hunts and banquets, but usually a demoniac fear of espionage suppressed such generous impulses. On journeys the foreign ambassadors had to accept the directions of their escort, which isolated them amid their Russian surroundings, spending the night for instance—and in winter, too—in the open instead of in the villages. In Moscow their attendants were charged, moreover, to prevent visits to the diplomatists' lodgings or, if such were approved, to be present at them.

Laborious as was the assemblage of his materials, information and experiences, Herberstein gave much thought to the relative importance to be attached to them. He was eager not only to bring nearer to his contemporaries a strange land known to them at best in only a fragmentary manner, but to replace the few superficial, wondrous and incredible accounts in circulation by a thorough and truthful description. It must be a real picture of all Russia. This was why he made contact with as many informants as he could, preferably independent of each other, comparing their reports among themselves and with his own observations. If there were no corroboration of some remarkable item and he were unable to substantiate it he would, however sensational it might be, leave it to the reader to judge for himself upon the evidence provided. Misunderstandings and mistakes have not been entirely eliminated despite so high a critical standard, but this scarcely reflects upon Herberstein if it is borne in mind that the scholarly study of Russia in Europe began with him.

Why with him? How had he come to learn Russian? What deeper motives prompted him to write a book of this character? How did he come to be selected for diplomatic missions in Moscow? These are questions which lead from the universally esteemed *Moscovia* to its almost unknown author.[1]

He owed his knowledge of Russian to his place of birth, Wippach (Vipava) in Carniola,[2] where his father, Leonhart, knight and incumbent of the captaincies of Adelsberg (Postojna in Slovene, Postumia in Italian) in the Carso and of Mitterburg (Pisino) in Istria, officiated as castellan of the former. Here Herberstein was born in 1486, scion of the indirect line of an ancient family from East Styria whose members, all vassals of the Emperor, sat here in the south-easternmost corner of the Empire facing the Venetians and the Turks. From Slovenes living in the Wippach district young Sigmund now laboriously learned Wendish—to his great advantage, for the then marked affinity of the Slavonic languages led on to his knowledge of Russian, Polish and Bohemian. We must not value it too highly, it is true; his Russian faltered at times, as his use of grammar in the *Moscovia* shows. He certainly knew the Cyrillic script but could not read it for long. Never-

[1] Concerning Herberstein cf. Friedrich Adelung, *Siegmund Freiherr von Herberstein*, St Petersburg, 1818, and my own Frankfurt doctoral thesis of 1962: *Das österreichische und osteuropäische Gesandtschaftwesen des 16. Jahrhunderts, untersucht an Sigmund von Herberstein*, which is provided with full references and documents.

[2] Former province east of Trieste and now part of Yugoslavia.

theless he could undertake simple conversations and even engage in etymological reflections.

His ability was far greater in Latin, which he knew as well as his German mother-tongue. He was a delicate child and thus, after attendance at the village school of Wippach, did not go on to knightly training as a page but received a scholar's education, first at the cathedral school of Gurk in Carinthia and then at the city school of St Stephen in Vienna. As a thirteen-year-old he enrolled in the faculty of philosophy at the University, becoming bachelor in 1502, and then spent two further years reading law. In these years at school and university Herberstein received a humanistic education which was to leave its stamp upon his personality, attainments and tastes for ever. He became a polished, quick-witted and convincing speaker, in Latin as well as German. Greek he could at least read; he had learned Italian in Wippach and could make himself understood in French and Spanish. He read the classics with avidity and was a good judge of antiquity. With no less concentration he took up the history of the later centuries, his survey ranging from Poland and Hungary to Italy and Spain, and was especially attracted by questions of genealogy. For the events of his own day, the period of the Reformation, he consulted even the works of Aventin and Sleidan without bothering about the frowns of authority towards these Protestant chroniclers. He liked to combine historical study with geographic inquiry and thereby found himself in a humanistic movement to which he was introduced by some of its leaders, such as Conrad Celtis whom he had met at the university. The impulse to write a work of the calibre of *Moscovia* springs from these early Viennese models and influences. Herberstein had other literary fields as well. The two most important works which he wrote, in German, together with a mass of other autobiographical and genealogical publications, were not, however, made public: his colourful and thrilling memoirs and the extensive and conscientious history of his family remained in manuscript and only for the perusal of the Herbersteins.

Although his education had begun with so much erudition Herberstein did not finally become a scholar. As a schoolboy he had had experience of knight service and of weapons and after his undergraduate years he made journeys with the imperial court; his earliest fame was achieved in his own part of the world by brave actions against the opposing Venetian troops. For this he was knighted by Maximilian in 1514 and summoned to service at court, and in the following year received his first diplomatic appointment.

For the next thirty-eight years, at longer or shorter intervals, there now followed one mission after the other. Herberstein set off on sixty-nine such errands at a period in which, in addition to the recently established permanent diplomatic representations, it was the custom to dispatch embassies with special tasks and time limits. He travelled across country as envoy of the Habsburgs, first of Maximilian but most of the time in the service of King, later Emperor, Ferdinand I. He made his way to the ecclesiastical and secular territories of the Empire, he knew Switzerland well, he went as far afield as Denmark and Spain. His orders took him most often to the countries of eastern Europe, to Poland, Bohemia and Hungary. In consequence of his recognized familiarity with conditions in the east it was to him that the two missions to Russia were entrusted. He ranks justly as the forerunner of the later Austrian experts on eastern Europe. He contributed vigorously to the stand which the house of Habsburg was making against the Reformation, to the resistance offered by Vienna to the growing aggression of the Turks, culminating in the first siege of the capital, to the securing of the Hungarian-Bohemian succession and thus to the momentous expansion of Austria to the east. He took part in the negotiations of German princes, of confederate assemblies and Hungarian parliaments, and was received by the Polish Kings Sigmund I and Sigmund II Augustus, by Emperor Charles V, the unfortunate King Ludwig II of Bavaria, the Grand-duke of Muscovy Basilius III, by Soleyman the Magnificent. Now it would be a treaty to be drawn up, now to remind allies of their promises. Or a peace to be made or an armistice arranged, whether for the benefit of his own country or on behalf of others. On formal occasions his absent monarch must be represented worthily. Political alliances were rivalled in importance—or so it was thought—by princely marriages: now Herberstein would be striving to arrange them, now negotiating the wedding-day and the extent of the dowry. He went to Nyköbing with the delicate task of inducing Christian II to abandon his mistress and return to his wife, a grand-daughter of

Charles V

the Emperor Maximilian. Herberstein sent current reports upon his business, often several times a day, in lively and explicit dispatches, often including other items arising in the place or country to which he had been sent. The burden of such work was linked to a deal of boring toil. The journeys that Herberstein made on horseback, by coach, in sledges or skiffs or sea-going boats, were arduous and sometimes protracted; he was nearly shipwrecked in the Mediterranean and was dismayed by the boggy, sandy, bridgeless main roads of the east. There were passports and safe-conducts, to be sure, and the diplomatist's right to independence, immunity and extra-territoriality was universally recognized, but every mission was nevertheless a dangerous enterprise. In many of the places to which he went to treat Herberstein was restricted in his movements through fear of spies or conspiracies, on several occasions he had to use weapons to ward off the attacks of highwaymen, and in Cracow he nearly became the victim of an attempt upon his life engineered by supporters of Johann Zapolyas, pretender to the throne of Hungary. It is not surprising that, like other diplomatists, he often felt sick of his profession. Once he even wrote to King Ferdinand saying that it was certainly his duty to serve the monarch, but with moderation, that he had often begged to be spared the many long, dangerous and arduous journeys but that the opposite had happened, that his fortune was gradually diminishing and that he scarcely ever saw his wife. He prayed that he might be relieved of his envoyships.

The Grand Turk Soleyman

This and other letters met with no success. Humbly and assiduously he went on carrying out his missions, although he was not a professional envoy for such did not yet exist, but appointed only *ad hoc*, his real sphere being that of the administration of the finances. He was a councillor in the Chamber of Lower Austria, his duties including, for instance, audits and the administration of justice, and was finally appointed its president. To this, his true vocation, he devoted all his energies; when age and illness prevented him from attending the sessions King Ferdinand ordered the other councillors to go to him in his home.

As financial expert and also member of the body which assisted the monarch in the most important affairs of state, the Privy Council, Herberstein distinguished himself as signally as in his capacity of ambassador or humanist or writer. The recognition he received on all sides was abundant and took many different forms. Maximilian gave him a house in Trieste, Ferdinand made over to him, together with all its rents, the fortified castle of Klamm, near Schottwien on the Semmering Pass, which he made his chief residence. Together with his brothers and cousins he was, finally, raised to the rank of baron after Charles V had granted him an achievement of his armorial bearings, which now included the bust of a Muscovite with sable hat, scourge and Tatar bow—a clear reference to his diplomatic efforts in Russia. The congratulations he received from unofficial sources vied with these honours and were certainly not directed solely at the author of *Moscovia*. As early as 1518, under the impact of the first mission to Russia, there had appeared in Cracow *Soteria*, a collection of Latin panegyrics made by the Polish diplomat and bishop of Ermland, Johann Dantiscus, in honour of Herberstein's achievements. A few years before his death a third and greatly augmented edition appeared which included a short account of his life in the guise of a hymn in prose. Further appreciations are to be found in many other contemporary books, and many an author or scholar dedicated his work respectfully to Herberstein.

But all this public recognition did not lead finally to the revelation of the personality of this dignified man with the long, deep scar upon his brow. His health was neither sound nor robust; he was both delicate and tough. His bearing was confident and well bred, which may have been why he was often appointed escort to exalted ladies. He was distinguished by his keen observation, to which were added good sense, knowledge of the world and an unerring and courageous firmness. He had marked self-confidence and *amour propre*, not on account of his aristocratic family but because he felt that he had lived worthily and thus merited his rank. He was proud of his cultured outlook, his professional and diplomatic successes, and recorded with gratification the praise lavished upon him. Whatever was due to him

The armorial bearings of Herberstein

he claimed and made no bones about it, such as for instance the monetary reward promised by some lofty lord for a useful service rendered. This desire to realize justified claims was so strong that it could lead him to methods which were unacceptable and even punishable. He gave proof of his humanity on many occasions, although at times he could be quite hard-hearted. He seems to have been an affectionate and attentive husband, as his letter to King Ferdinand suggests, and brought back to his wife Helene, née Graswein and the widow of von Saurau, many a present. He had no children, a great affliction, for his was a thoroughly instructive nature and he took a keen interest in education; his little nephews turned to him for every kind of guidance. His attitude to religion, a revealing point in any contemporary of the Reformation, was unquestionably that of a believer. He had himself taken part in decisive measures in the cleavage of the faiths and he knew the representatives and concerns of the Protestants from his own experience. He certainly remained on the side of the established Church, but watchfully and critically. He read the publications of evangelical theologians and historians and wished that the two creeds could get along together, and this attitude evidently did him no harm.

Herberstein's own translation into German of his book on Russia, virtually a definitive edition as regards the contents, forms the basis of the selection offered here. The selection is confined to the heart of the book, the portrayal of Russia, and passages about Lithuania, Scandinavia and other places have been omitted. But even the description of Russia has been abridged, e.g. in the treatment of Russian history and in several chapters about the Orthodox faith. The goal aimed at has been to retain those longer and shorter passages, arranged according to subject, which seemed likely to offer a general impression of Herberstein's work and thus of sixteenth-century Russia. The somewhat fanciful German of this contemporary of Luther has been adjusted to modern usage but retained whenever the vocabulary and construction of today permitted. Russian words which Herberstein sprinkled in his pages in more or less distorted shape are given in the transliteration of their present form: thus *Knyaz* instead of *Knes*. The same procedure has been followed with proper, and especially, place names: thus Vorotynsk rather than Herberstein's Worotin. If he uses the Latin form it has been retained but supplemented by the Russian, e.g. Tanais (Don). Such adjustments may serve to clarify the intention of this selection: intelligibility and as close a preservation of the original text as possible.

It is with pleasure that I undertake the obligation of offering my thanks for the manifold help given in my work: to the Austrian National Library, Vienna, the Bavarian State Library, Munich, the State Library of the Preussischer Kulturbesitz Foundation in Marburg, the University Libraries of Erlangen, Frankfurt, Graz and Würzburg, the Austrian Domestic, Court and State Archives, Vienna. I am especially grateful to the Austrian Foreign Policy and International Relations Society, their Research Director and their Secretary-General, Dr Meraviglia, for making the appearance of this book possible. I would like to thank Professor Verosta for his essay[1], and to make mention also of the patient assistance of my wife.

One acknowledgment comes unfortunately too late. It is that to Professor Karl Braunias, ambassador and minister plenipotentiary, who supervised the first two volumes of *The Austrian Diplomats* series and gave much interest and many fresh ideas to this, the third. His death in August 1965 prevented him from reading the completed manuscript version sent to Vienna shortly after. The dedication of the book to his memory will show how much it owes to him.

1969. BERTOLD PICARD.

[1] See page 98.

I

BASIS AND PURPOSE OF THIS WORK

'. . . *And I have sought to set forth and describe it for posterity not in lofty terms but common German words.*'

The name of the capital of the Russians in Scythia, whose princes' power and territory stretches far and wide, is Moscow (Moskau) in both German and Russian, but in Latin it is Moscovia. To describe it I must mention many places in the North which were not well known to our forefathers, even those who have written of them in our own day. If my account does not always tally with theirs it is not because I wished to exalt myself and belittle them, but because I was sent thither as ambassador first of the Emperor Maximilian and the second time upon the order of the most gracious Ferdinand, Roman Majesty and Lord of Hungary and Bohemia etc., and have seen the land and city of Moscow and much of their manners and customs. Most of what I have written comes not from the narrations of one informant nor a dozen but from the consistent accounts of many persons met and encountered during these two journeys, in which I was much helped by my knowledge of the Wendish tongue, also called in Latin by the Russian name of Slavonic and resembling the speech of Russia or Muscovy. Thus I can bear witness not merely from hearsay but as one who has seen partly for himself, and I have sought to set forth and describe it for posterity not in lofty terms but common German words.

II

THE COUNTRY

'Here follows the description of the principalities and domains of the Grand-duke of Moscow, and first of Moscow itself. From there I proceed to the most considerable and renowned dominions, as far as I could learn of them by thorough inquiry and experience. Thus the reader must rest content with some only of these towns and rivers and mountains.'

I GENERAL SURVEY

The Slavonic or Wendish tongue, now commonly but not rightly called Sclavonic, is widespread and spoken by the Dalmatians, Bosnians, Croats and Istrians. Its use stretches up the Adriatic Sea as far as Friuli. This tongue is spoken also by the Carniolans,[1] called in Latin the Carni and in the Venetian and Italian tongues Carssi, and further by the Ukrainians and the Carinthians as far as the River Drava, by the Styrians to four leagues below Graz, then following the Mur down to the Danube. Thereafter, on the far side of the Drava and the Save, by the Mysians, Serbs, Bulgars and other peoples until close by Constantinople. Then come the Bohemians, the Lusatians, Silesians, Moravians; the Wends along the Vah and many of the peoples between the Vah and Hungary; the Poles, the Russians and further the Circassians called of the Five Mountains who dwell by the Black Sea, called Pontus Euxinus in Latin. Some have wandered towards the Elbe and have scattered villages there; these are the survivors of the Wends who lived within this region. All of them declare themselves Slav. It is the German custom to name all who speak the Slavonic tongue Wends or Wendish without distinction. The Moldavians and other

[1] Slovenes in and around Udine.

Wallachians living hard by employ this tongue similarly in writings and in church services although they have another common speech.

The Latin 'Russia' is called Russland in German. There are many opinions about the origin of this name. Some tell of Russo, brother of the Polish Prince Lech, who is said to have become prince of the Russians and from whom the name was taken or handed on. Others think the name came from an ancient place or settlement (*staraja*) called Russa, situated not far from Novgorod; others again that it came from the dark brown skin of this people. Many hold that the name Roxolania was used in Russia. All such opinions imply that Russia was not firmly settled and observe that Russia was formerly called Rosseya, meaning in their language a scattered people. This they seek to support with the fact that their nation never lives entirely by itself and is everywhere mingled with others. From whoever the name of Russia may have come it is that of all the Russians who use the Wendish or Slavonic tongue and observe the Christian beliefs and ceremonies of the Greek Church as laid down. In their own language they are called Russy, in Latin Ruthenians and in German Russen, and have grown so greatly in number that they have either expelled all the peoples with whom they have intermixed or compelled them to adopt their own customs, so that all in common are now called Russians. Russia reaches close to the Carpathian mountains not far from Cracow and follows the River Tyras, which the natives of these parts call the Dniester, down to the Pontus Euxinus, otherwise called the Black or in Italian the Greater Sea, and then over to the water of the Borysthenes, or Dnieper in Russian.

Now some years ago the Turks captured Weissenburg (Belgorod-Dniestrovski), also known as Mauro Castro, which had belonged to the voivods of Moldavia and is situated at the mouth of the River Dniester. There the Tatar king of Perekop in Russian, Taurida in Latin, had attacked across the Dnieper, laying waste far and wide, and built two castles. One of them, called Otshakov, lies not far from the mouth of the Dniester and is also in Turkish hands now. Thus it comes about that even today there are large tracts of devastated land between the Dniester and the Dnieper stretching down to the sea. The traveller who follows the Dnieper upstream reaches Russia again near Cherkassy, lying to the west; from there he approaches Kanev and Kiev, anciently the capital of the Russians and seat of the princes and the government. Across the Dnieper here is the duchy of Severian, still with its residence and garrison. He who then travels directly eastward from there comes to the source of the famous Tanais (Don) and, far beyond this river, to the confluence of the Oka and the Volga, called Rha in Greek. Here Russia stretches out beyond the Volga towards the north and, if one finishes the circuit, it extends to the countries in obedience to the King of Sweden and even to Finland, to Livonia (Latvia), Samogitia, Masuria and then back to Poland and along its boundary down to the Sarmatian Mountains.

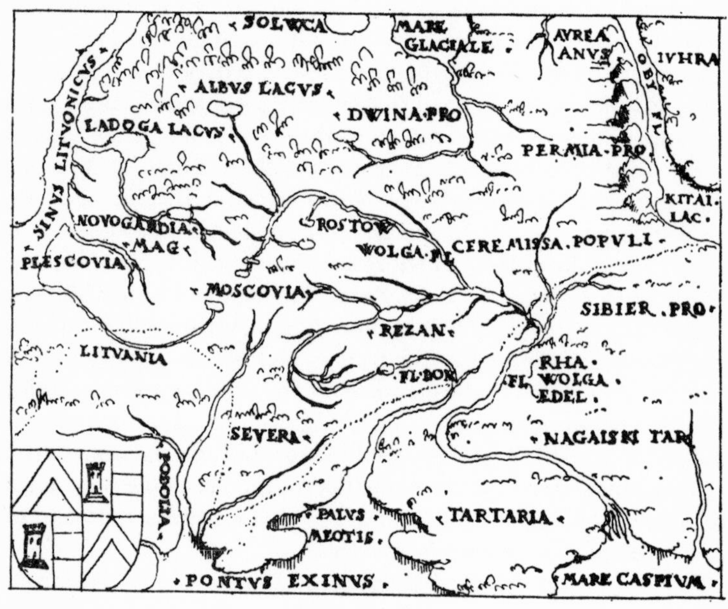

Muscovy

In this whole area two countries are exceptions: Lithuania and Samogitia,[1] which adhere to the Roman ritual and have each their own language. Nevertheless there are many subjects in these principalities and in Lithuania, even in its capital of Vilna, who are Russians. There are now three princes of the Russians. The first is the Prince of Moscow, lord of most of the realm; the second is the Grand-duke of Lithuania; and the third is the King of Poland. For all that, Poland and Lithuania have but one ruler at the present.

[1] Formerly a province of Lithuania and once independent.

2 LANDSCAPE AND SETTLEMENTS

Here follows the description of the principalities and domains of the Grand-duke of Moscow, and first of Moscow itself. From there I set forth to the most considerable and renowned duchies, as far as I could learn of them by thorough inquiry and travel. Thus the reader must rest content with some only of the towns and rivers and mountains.

Moscow the town, capital of Russia, the principality of the same name and the River Moskva which traverses the city all bear the same name without distinction. Which one gave it to the others I do not know. Yet it may be supposed that, as in many places, the river bore it first. Albeit the town had no great prominence hitherto its name was nevertheless known to the ancients.

The River Moskva has its source in the duchy of Tver or Otwer seventy *versts* above Mozhaisk (a verst is as much as a Western league), not far from a place called Oleshko. Having flowed ninety versts it reaches the town of Moscow, moves on to the east and joins the Oka. From six leagues above Mozhaisk timber for building and other needs is floated down to the city. Below Moscow the river is navigable, so that merchandise and other goods can be shipped in both directions. But the journey is very slow because of the detours of the river, especially between Moscow and the town of Kolomna lying three thousand paces from the mouth of the stream: these loops amount to two hundred and seventy versts. The Moskva is ill stocked with fish.

The principality bearing this name is in itself neither great nor extensive, nor yet notably fertile. (. . .) The cold is often so extreme that the earth, as with us in hot weather, swells and splits. When one throws water up into the air in such great cold it freezes before it reaches the ground. On our recent visit here we saw branches of fruit trees ruined by the frost of the previous year. We were told also that certain post-boys, whom they call *gonez*, having laid themselves in the sledges and been driven by another to the posting relay, were found frozen to death. Nor is this all. When certain gentlemen had sent for cattle to be slaughtered at their farms the servant of one of them was leading an ox and had tied the halter round his arm; he was found frozen in a sitting posture, and the ox as well. Some who went about with dancing bears froze also, upon which the bears went to the houses and broke in the gates, frightening some poor folk so that they and their children fled and froze likewise. On the other hand it also happens that there is intemperate heat, as in the year 1525. (. . .) Crops in the fields, forests and houses, were kindled and burned by the great heat alone. From this came such boundless smoke into the land that many lost the full use of their eyes and many were blinded.

Like the others in this duchy the town lies well to the east, for usually upon our journey the morning sun shone into our eyes against us; though not in Asia the place is hard upon its borders.

Moscow is very large and appears even larger from a distance. It is built entirely of wood. For this reason the artisans, most of whom have fire at hand, are all outside the town and there is a long row of buildings beyond it. In between lie large squares, making the city look larger than it is. Other dwellings lie not far from the town, and across the water lies a well enclosed township inhabited by foreign soldiers. It is called Nali, meaning in their tongue something like 'pour out' or 'fill up', for the reason that though mead and beer are generally forbidden to the common man it is allowed to these as warriors. From this has come the name. There are also several convents outside the city, looking like towns seen from afar. The town is not protected by walls or ditches or battlements. Some of the lanes have barriers or gates, shut at night at fixed hours so that their passage is not open to all and sundry, some of whom might wish to harm other people. A stranger who crosses the barriers is struck down and stripped, or taken to prison. Such precautions are laid down for the general security. Beyond, the River Moskva flows through the town, and directly beneath it is the Jausa brook. This is fortified to some height and has few crossings. It has many mills and it empties into the Moskva. The city is, save for a few convents, churches and houses, built entirely of wood. They told us that the Prince had had the houses counted six years ago and found there were forty-one thousand five hundred of them. As the ground is sandy the streets and lanes are woefully pitted and hence the most respectable lanes and spaces are bridged over.

The castle's walls are faced with tiles. One side of it lies along the Moskva, the other along the Neglinka brook which flows hither from a marsh not far away. It is barred close to the castle and then looks like a moat or pond, with mills at its outflow. It falls into the Moskva above the castle. From its size it could be called a townlet, for many walled apartments of the Grand-duke's lie within. The Metropolitan and his priests, the brothers of the Grand-duke, many of the councillors and the Prince's artisans have their houses here. There are two fine churches here, well built and ornamented, those of Our Lady and St Michael, as well as other churches of which two, at the time that we were there, were being walled.

The Grand-duke John (Ivan I Kalita) was the first to build and wall

The Grand-duke Basilius III

the castle; before the time of Ivan, son of the Grand-duke Daniel, all was made wretchedly of wood. It was on the advice and admonition of Peter, the Metropolitan, who was a profound admirer of Alexius, buried there and said to have performed several miracles, that Ivan built his princely seat in this place. At his death such wonders are said to have taken place at his tomb, causing such reverence for its site, that all the succeeding grand-dukes have had their seat there. After this John they speak of his son, also John (Ivan II, the Handsome), then of Demetrius (Dimitri Donskoi); after him of Basilius (Vassili II) the Blind, father of John the Great (Ivan III) who was in turn father of Basilius III, previously called Gabriel. The castle took thirty years to complete. It was built in their own style by westerners brought in at great cost. In the Chapel of Our Lady lie the two of them, Alexius and Peter the Miracle-Worker; in the other church the princes lie buried.

Within the memory of man no fatality nor plague such as has been suffered elsewhere has been brought here along the Tanais (Don) from the east or north. None the less they have cramp of the bowels and aching of the head; they call them *vretiye*, signifying heat or hot, and often perish. At the time we were there many of them died of it, even one of our own following. Thus when the plague is raging at Novgorod or Pskov or Smolensk they forbid those from these places to enter the city or even the duchy.

The people of Moscow are far more crafty and deceitful than those around them. Being now aware that others are mistrustful of them they do not discover themselves willingly, calling themselves strangers and belying their citizenship.

The longest day of the year in Moscow has eighteen and three quarter hours of light. I could not find out the latitude, though some say fifty-eight degrees, and at noon on the eighth day of June I beheld the sun at this degree. Those skilled in this art reckoned therefrom that the latitude was only fifty degrees [1] and the day of only seventeen and a quarter hours.

Now that I have told of Moscow I shall continue eastward, then to the south and on to the west and north.

Vladimir comes first, a large town with a castle of wood which the princes have made their seat from the time of St Vladimir,[2] christened Basilius, down to that of Ivan I Kalita, son of Daniel. It lies between the two great waters of the Volga and the Oka, thirty-six leagues from Moscow, in a very fertile place where often a single measure of corn will yield twenty or thirty. It is watered by the Klyazma river, and very great forests surround it on all sides. The Klyazma rises four leagues from Moscow and has many mills beside it. Ships carry the traveller from below the town along this stream to Murom on the Oka, lying twenty-four leagues eastward of Vladimir and reached through great

[1] It is in fact 55·45°.
[2] In fact only from the time of Andrei Bogulyubski.

forests. It was once a duchy and its people were called Muromani; they were once rich in honey, wax, hides and fish.

Nizhniy Novgorod (now Gorki) is a large wooden town with a castle of stone and masonry built by Basilius (Vassili III) upon a rock at the confluence of the Volga and the Oka, and said to lie forty leagues from Murom. Be this distance what it may, Novgorod must be a hundred leagues from Moscow. The fertility of the land is likened to that of Vladimir. Here Christendom comes to an end. Although the Grand-duke has another castle farther down called Sura there are tribes between, the Czeremissi, who are not Christian but Mohammedan, as well as other tribes called the Mordvins. These people live upon the right bank of the Volga, going downstream, the Czeremissi upon the other side towards the north. There are also Czeremissi near to Novgorod, called the upper or of the mountains. Nevertheless there are no mountains, but there are hills; their name may come from these. The River Sura separates the Muscovite territory from the kingdom of Kazan; it flows from the south, and twenty-eight leagues below Novgorod turns east and empties into the Volga. Basilius built a castle at the confluence, naming it Vassil-Sursk after himself. Close by is a river called the Moshka, coming also from the south; it joins the Oka above Murom not far from Kassimov, which the Grand-duke once gave the Tatars to inhabit.

From the Moshka towards the east and south are great forests everywhere in which the Mordvin peoples dwell; they have their own tongue and are subject to the Grand-duke. Some say they are Mohammedans, but others heathen. They have villages and till the soil, living mainly on venison and honey. They have many good hides too. They are a hardy race; they have bows and are well skilled in their use, they have often sent the Tatars about their business: all this is done on foot. Ryazan, an ancient ducal seat between the Oka and the Tanais (Don), is of wood and lies not far from the banks of the Oka. Formerly it had a castle called Jaroslav, of which the site and some remnants may be seen. Not far from the town the Oka has an island called Strub, and this duchy was free and subject to none. For this reason its lords were also called grand-dukes. On the way hither from Moscow, keeping midway between east and south (which some call towards winter), the traveller comes to the town of Kolomna, a ride of thirty-six German leagues according to the versts.

The merchant who travels from Moscow to the River Tanais (Don) to load merchandise upon the boats will follow the road to Ryazan, and twenty-four leagues beyond it he will reach this river again at a place called Dankov. From there he and the ships travel down to Azov, emerging from the river into the sea, called in Latin the marsh of Palus Maeotis (Sea of Azov), and onward to Kaffa (Fedorovka) and Constantinople beyond. This loading of the ships takes place commonly in the autumn if the year has been rainy, for the Tanais has not always at these places a sufficiency of water for ships.

Tula, a town lying some forty leagues from Ryazan and a ride southward from Moscow of thirty-six leagues, is the last place before the desert. Basilius (Vassili III) built a walled castle there, which I visited. Past it flows the stream called Tula (Tulitza), whilst from the east comes the River Upa running past the castle. The two waters join and then fall into the Oka some twenty leagues upstream of Vorotinsk, not far from which confluence stands the castle of Odojevo. Tula once had its own prince.

The Tanais (Don), that celebrated river which is called a frontier between Europe and Asia, has its source eight leagues south of Tula. For a short distance it flows eastward from a lake called Ivan-Osyero, or John's Lake—not from the Riphey Mountains, as so many of the ancients have written. Two great waters flow from this lake. The first course of the Tanais lies eastward, later between Kazan and Astrakhan it comes within six or seven leagues of the great River Volga and there turns south and so reaches the sea called Maeotis (Azov). The other stream is the Shat, which flows west. The Upa joins the Shat and both flow north-west into the Oka. The nearest town to the source of the Tanais is Upa; and some three leagues above the estuary of this same Tanais lies Azov, a great town which is said once to have been called Tanais.

The roads and journeys to these places are reckoned not in versts or leagues but in days' travel. Since they count thirty versts or by my reckoning six leagues to a day's journey, it is thus about eighty German leagues overland from the source of the Tanais to its estuary. But travelling by water, and starting at Dankov, one barely reaches Azov in twenty days. The town, paying tribute to the Turks, is five days distant from Perekop. Though much has been written about the altars of Alexander the Great I have not been able to discover that the slightest glimpse is to be had of them. I have talked with and questioned those who have often travelled through these places, and they replied that they had neither seen nor ever heard of them. There is a river called the little Tanais (Donetz), and where it joins the real Tanais (Don) three days' journey above Azov they speak of certain marbles, pillars and sculptures to be found there at the place named Veliki Perevos, called In the Sacred Mountains. The Little Tanais rises in the land of Severia and is thus called the Severski Donetz. Travellers from Moscow to Azov pass through Dankov and then turn slightly east. Hence if a line were drawn from the estuary to the source of the Tanais and projected northward it might be said that Moscow lies in Asia and not in Europe. Mtsensk lies in marshy ground, none the less there was a castle there as certain remains testify. Of late there were people living there in huts who, when the enemy threatened, took flight into the marshes. From Moscow to this place you go southward about sixty leagues. From Tula it is some thirty.

The Oka, the river already mentioned, rises about eighteen leagues from Mtsensk. Its first course is eastward, then it moves north and again towards sunrise, as they term it, almost encircling Mtsensk. There are many towns upon this river, such as Cherpuchov, Voroyinsk, Kaluga, Kashira, Kolomna, Ryazan, Kassimov and Murom, and it joins the Volga below Nizhne Novgorod. It has many forests on each bank from which honey, minivers, ermine and martens are procured. All the land watered by this river is productive, especially there are finer fish than any others in the vicinity of Moscow and notable are those caught near Murom. In it too are taken fish called *byeluga* which have no bones, but only gristle, like sturgeons; they have a great head and a mouth like a scabbard and are called *waller* in certain places. Then come Ruthenian sharks, *sevryuga* and *osetr*, which might be three variants of sturgeon, beadle-fish, and *Dück* (as we call them). Then there is *belorybiza*, a white fish with bright, silvery scales, and very good to eat. It is believed that all these fish come from the Volga, and thence from the sea, save for the white fish.

The town of Kaluga lies upon the Oka thirty-six leagues from Moscow and fourteen from Cherpuchov. Here are fine woodwork, bowls, drinking vessels and the like. They are sent forth from here to Moscow, Lithuania and other places. Every year the prince rallies his people against the attack of the Tatars.

Vorotinsk, with principality, town and castle of the same name, lies three leagues above Kaluga and not far from the banks of the Oka. Earlier the principality was in the hands of Knyaz Ivan Borotinski, a valiant and seasoned warrior through whom Grand-duke Basilius (Vassili III) won many victories over his enemies. (. . .)

Severia is a grand-duchy in which was the seat of the former princes,

Novgorod Severski. Bearing westward the traveller goes south from Moscow through Kaluga, Vorotinsk, Serensk and Briansk for a hundred and fifty German leagues. Severia stretches as far as the Dnieper and has many wastes; at Briansk there is a very great forest. In this land are many castles and towns: Starodub, Putivl, Chernigov are the most important. It is a fertile country well stocked with honey, ermine, minivers and martens. The people are good soldiers from their daily sallies against the Tatars.

The journey from Putivl towards Perekop, called Taurica in Latin, is through waste lands and across the rivers Sula, Samara and Orel; the last two are broader and deeper and travellers crossing the streams are often upset. Hereafter one reaches the rivers Konskaya and Molochnaya. In these places they hew branches from the trees and tie them in bundles. Passengers and their goods are placed upon these and pushed off so that, with a little help, they float across to the other shore. Some travellers tie such bundles to their horses' tails and drive them into the water, swimming as they lead them across. The Ugra, a deep and muddy watercourse, rises not far from Dorogobuzh in a forest lying between Kaluga and Vorotinsk and falls into the Oka. Formerly it was the boundary between Lithuania and the Muscovy land.

Smolensk is the name of both a castle and a town. What is not enclosed is called the town. But that which is walled in, for Smolensk is a great fortress with many buildings and encompassed with wood and stone and ramparts, is known as Gorod, the common Wendish for a castle but interpreted as one which has its *enceinte*.

Smolensk is the seat of both a prince and a bishop. It lies upon the renowned Dnieper, or Borysthenes in Latin. The castle lies across the water on a slope and upon the top of the hillock is the walled church of Our Lady; the rest is of wood. Around the castle is a ditch, not much over knee-deep, into which stakes have been driven like those of the Austrian vineyards save that these are shorter, stronger and narrower. They are to ward off attackers. It is reported that Basilius (Vassili III) could not win the place by force of arms and gained it through the surrenders of the vassals. But the many houses of what is called the town are between the knolls across the river. Close to the town are sundry walls where convents once stood.

The principality lies amid great forests yielding hides and especially good honey. Towards Dubrovno the woods are filled with lime-trees on which the bees feed and make their excellent honey.

The road from Moscow to Smolensk lies between south and west. First comes Mozhaisk after eighteen leagues, Vyazma twenty-six leagues farther on, Dorogobuzh eighteen beyond and then another eighteen to Smolensk. This comes to eighty leagues, although both the Lithuanians and Muscovites speak of a hundred; I have travelled this road three times and not found it more than eighty. The principality was taken in 1413 by Vitold or Vitovd (both forms are cited), a Lithuanian grand-duke by birth, from one of the Basils (Vassili I), who later carried off his daughter. Basilius (Vassili III) recaptured it on the thirteenth day of July in 1514 in the time of King Sigismund of Poland, Grand-duke of Lithuania.

Dorogobuzh and Vyazma, their wooden castles and towns lying along the Dnieper, were both formerly under Lithuania. Not far from Vyazma flows a stream of this name which joins the Dnieper about two versts from the town. It is here that ships are laden for Smolensk and to here that they return, just as our own baggage lately made this voyage up and down stream. Mozhaisk and its princely seat are also all of wood. Here the prince has held his annual sports and coursing; there is an abundance of hares of various colours, the like of which I have never seen. (. . .) Near to Mozhaisk, about six leagues towards Moscow, the Lithuanian boundary stood in Vitold's time.

Belyi is another principality with castle and town and on a stream called the Obsha, running between great forests. It is sixty leagues from Moscow, towards the west and slightly south, thirty-six from Smolensk and thirty from Toropets. The princes who formerly lived there were descended from Ghedimin (of Lithuania) and formerly loyal to the Lithuanians. But in the time of Casimir, King of Poland and Grand-duke of Lithuania, Basilius Prince of Belyi (from which the inhabitants have their name of Belski) submitted to John (Ivan III), Grand-duke of Moscow, and abandoned the young wife already mentioned. His elder son Dimitri was held in high esteem in our own day but the principality has been kept by the Grand-duke, who includes it in his title.

The town and castle of Rzhev lie twenty-three leagues due west of Moscow. The castle from which the prince takes his title lies upon the great and famous River Volga, written as Rha in ancient books, and he rules over a large and extensive territory. (. . .)

He who walks a few leagues westward from Rzhev comes to the Forest of Volkonski, from which four notable waters flow. Here is a swamp called Fronovo. From it comes a brook which falls after barely two leagues into a lake called the Volgo. Somewhat larger the brook flows out of it, now bearing the name of Volga; it flows through many marshes and lakes and is swelled by many tributaries. It runs eastward and falls into the sea which the Muscovites call Hvalinskoy and the Latins Caspium and Hyrcanum; some say it has twenty-five branches, others seventy. The Tatars, whose land it often crosses, call it the Noble. This river and the Tanais (Don) come in one place within seven leagues, as has already been told.

Near Fronovo, the marsh, is a village called Dnieprovo close to which rises the Dnieper, the river known in Latin as Borysthenes. Close at hand is the convent of the Holy Trinity where lies the source of a stream called the Dnieperez, or Little Dnieper, yet which is larger than the former. The two brooks join and soon become navigable. Here the ships are laden with wares brought by the merchants of Kholopigorod and carried into Lithuania. The traders' quarters are close by the convent. From merchants and others who have traded and travelled in these parts I have learned to my own satisfaction that the Rha or Volga and the Borysthenes or Dnieper do not share a common source, as some have written. The first course of the Dnieper is southward towards Vyazma, where it turns slightly east towards Dorogobuzh, Smolensk, Orscha and Mogilev, bearing then southward again to Kiev, Cherkassy, Ochakov and falling into the Black Sea or Pontine in Latin. As the river reaches the sea it broadens out like a lake, whence many have deceived themselves into saying that it ends in a lake, as was formerly believed.

When we travelled from Orscha up to Smolensk we loaded our baggage upon a ship making for close by Vyazma, but landed in Smolensk for Easter. After the melting of the snow the streams were greatly swollen, and a monk at one of the convents took the Count (Nogarola) and me in a skiff through the flooded forests back to our course. Here we waited until our saddles and suchlike were brought to us in the same skiff. But three or four times the horses had to swim from one knoll to the next. For there are many hillocks along the Dnieper and between any two of them there flows a brook. Because of the flooding of the Dnieper these had become so wide that the horses were forced to swim.

The Dvina is a lake ten leagues from the source of the Dnieper and as far from Fronovo. Here rises a stream of the same name turning west and running to within twenty leagues of Vilna. Then it turns north and at Riga, capital of Latvia, empties into the German or

Latvian Sea, which the Russians call Varyaskoy. It flows through Vitebsk and Polotsk, not touching Pskov as a writer has said but moving towards Dvinsk (Daugavpils). This belongs to the Latvians and takes its name from the river, which they call the Dvina or Duna. On my first journey I travelled more than twelve leagues upstream towards Polotsk in a sledge. There was one place where water stretched from shore to shore without ice, but the narrow track had been hardened by the traffic and held firm between the upper and lower layers of ice, being about five paces broad. This is the compass of the common sledges. My men and I traversed this passage, God be praised, though not without anxiety.

The Lovat, the fourth of the rivers, is not to be likened to the others in size. It rises between the Dvina lake and Fronovo; actually it rises north-west of Smolensk or even from the same marsh; I was not able to find out precisely. The Russians record that St Andrew, when he had reached the source of the Dnieper or Borysthenes, voyaged down the Lovat to Novgorod. After forty leagues this water comes to Velikie Luki, passing on then to Lake Ilmen.

Velikie Luki, castle and town, lies a hundred and forty leagues [1] west from Moscow, some sixty from Novgorod, sixty-three from Polotsk. It is upon the regular route from Moscow to Lithuania.

Tver or Otwer (now Kalinin) is a grand-duchy with formerly extensive territory. It lies on the Volga thirty-six leagues west of Moscow. The wooden castle lies upon the bank nearer to Moscow; the town and many other houses stand upon both shores. Opposite the castle the river is joined by a tributary called the Tverza, upon which I took ship on my first Volga voyage. On the following day I seated myself in a larger vessel, expecting to travel some miles down the Volga. But when we had scarcely covered one league we saw the ice stretching across from bank to bank at one of the bends. With much toil and effort we had to lift the great thick blocks of ice which lay upon the bank and slide them down so that we could approach the shore and get out. We went to a convent, that of St Elias, and waited some hours until horses were brought. (. . .)

The name of Great Novgorod, where formerly the Russian princes had their seat and court, signifies in Russian Newtown or Newcastle. For as already mentioned, whatever is walled or fortified they call Gorod. It is a large and extensive town, though circumvallated only in part.

[1] Unless the road was very indirect the figure seems too high. Today it is under three hundred miles.

Through it flows the Volkhov, rising out of Lake Ilmen two versts above the town. It is navigable and ends in a lake formerly called Veva but now named Ladoga after the small town which lies there. From Moscow the journey hither is to the west and of a hundred and twenty leagues, or according to some only one hundred; the town lies thirty-six leagues from Pskov and forty from Velikie Luki, the same from Ivangorod (Narva).

Before its subjection the town commanded a large and extensive territory, principally to the north and east, which was divided into five parts. Each had in the town itself its own magistracy, which gave judgments and decisions in public and private matters. Nothing went beyond this magistracy. At the time of which I write much trade was done there, and great stocks of goods held, by merchants of every land, bringing great wealth. During my visit there were German merchants' dealers or factors in the town who begged from me as a memento a sleigh which I had brought from Augsburg, and had it put in the church.

They had as neighbours Latvians, Finns and others from the coasts under the Swedish obedience, including the Norwegians. Novgorod had subsidiary grand-duchies attached to it, such as Dvina and Vologda to the east and Torshok to the south. Because of the many forests and waters such domains cannot be well known, yet they make much profit from game, smoked meats, honey, wax and abundant fish.

The rulers of this place have courted sedulously the friendship and goodwill of their neighbours, gaining also their protection with large gifts. From this comes the boasting of the Muscovites, as though they had always had their own regents in charge at Novgorod; whilst the Lithuanians maintain that its inhabitants had been their own tributaries or vassals.

A much respected archbishop ruled here firmly for some time. Grand-duke John (Ivan III) waged war against these people for seven years before defeating them in the autumn of 1477 by the Shelon river. With some reservations they submitted and accepted a governor. But since Grand-duke John's power over them was not yet absolute and he could not hope to obtain this without recourse to arms he hit upon the expedient of alleging that the Novgorodans were seeking to change their faith, and came there with his army as though to maintain it. He entered forthwith into the city which he took into perpetual bondage, and stripped the archbishop, citizens, merchants and foreigners of all they had. I was told by many persons how he drove off to Moscow with more than three hundred wagons laden with gold, silver, jewels, valuables and other booty, as well as with the archbishop and some of the townspeople. Keeping them in Moscow and making the prelate a liberal allowance, he gave their houses to others and set up a new bishop, allotting him but a small part of this income. After his death the province had for long no bishop, until the Grand-duke sent one upon the petition of the citizens and community.

In distant times Novgorod had an idol called Perun, standing in a place where there is now a convent named thereafter, Perunski. When the citizens accepted Christian baptism they cast the idol into the River Volkhov. They say that it moved upstream and that a voice was heard by the bridge saying: 'Take this, Novgorodans, in memory of me!', upon which a cudgel was flung upon the bridge. A voice is still heard several times a year crying: 'Perun, Perun.' The throng gathers and they attack each other with sticks and fists; there is a great commotion, which the authorities find it hard to quieten.

Their chronicles tell that the Novgorodans journeyed to Greece and besieged the Chersonesus for seven years. Their women gave up hope of their menfolk and took their serfs as husbands. When the Chersonesus had been won and the men came home they brought with them a door and bell of copper as tokens of their victory. They showed me such a door in the church at Novgorod, and the bell is said to hang in the tower. The vassals met their masters upon the field of battle and won the first round. One of the latter is said to have counselled his fellows to fight the vassals not with arms but with cudgels and lashes: these would remind them of their former servitude and lower their spirits. Thus it happened, and the serfs fled. Arriving at a place still called today Kholopigorod (signifying the stronghold or place of the servants), they were overcome and put to death grievously. The wives hanged themselves.

The longest day in the year at Novgorod has eighteen hours and more. But it is a very cold place, worse than Moscow. The people are said to have been worthy and compassionate folk, but have become very mixed.

Lake Ilmen, often found in old Russian books and writings as Ilmer, and called by some of the Latins Limidis, lies two versts above Novgorod. It is twelve leagues long and eight broad. Apart from other small ones, it is joined by two rivers, the Lovat and the Shelon which itself rises in a lake. But only one river flows out of Lake Ilmen, the Volkov, flowing through Novgorod and onward for six and thirty leagues before it falls into Lake Ladoga, as described earlier. This Lake Ladoga is reckoned to be a hundred leagues long and sixty broad; none the less it has various patches of land and eyots within it. Out of it flows a great stream called the Neva, running westward and falling then into the Lithuanian or Finnish Gulf. At its mouth the Muscovite princes have a castle called Oreshek in their tongue and Nitenburg (Schlüsselburg) in German.

(Staraya) Russa is an ancient principality and was formerly called Old Russia. It lies within the district of Novgorod and is twelve leagues distant from the town, but thirteen from the lake. It has a salty water which the citizens collect in a pit like a pond. They carry this water thence to their houses in pipes and boil it to deposit the salt.

Ivangorod (Narva) was given his own name by Grand-duke John and built on the bank of the River Narva. It is walled. Opposite the castle and also on the bank is the Latvian castle, called after the Narva; this river is the boundary between the two domains. It comes out of the lake they call Chudskoy, in Latin Bicis or Pelas, in German Peipus (Peipsi). Two rivers flow into this lake, the Pskova and the Velikaya. The latter comes from the south, flowing past Opotscha where I crossed it by the first floating bridge, and leaves the town of Pskov upon the right hand. You cannot pass from Pskov right into the sea because of the steep rocks and falls of water close to Ivangorod.

Pleskau, also known as Pskov, is a notable town lying upon a lake. Out of it comes a stream of the same name as the town which flows through the latter and then, after six leagues, into Lake Peipsi. This is the only walled town in all the Muscovite territory and is divided into four separate quarters. Many have therefore said that the town had four walls around it. In former times it was called Pskov and Obskov; it had much land and became a free city. (. . .)

I shall now describe the towns and rivers along the sea coast from here unto Sweden. (. . .)

Carelia (not the place of which I have already told) is a vast land which has its own tongue and lies some sixty leagues north of Novgorod. And although the inhabitants receive tribute from some of their neighbours, they pay out no less in tribute to the King of Sweden and the Grand-duke of Moscow than does the Lord of Novgorod.

Solovetski is an island to the north between the lands of Dvina and Carelia and lying eight leagues from the coast of the White Sea. I was not able to learn how far it is from Moscow, for there are so many bare forests, marshes and obstacles in these parts. It is nevertheless held commonly to be three hundred leagues, though only two hundred from Byelozersk. Much salt is panned upon this island, and there is a monastery into which no woman may go. There is much fishing of the *selgi*, which are thought to be herring. They say too that the sun shines for but two hours upon the short days.

Dmitrov, with castle and town, is twelve leagues north by west of Moscow. It was given to the Grand-duke's brother George for his maintenance. The stream there is called the Yachroma and joins the Syestra; this falls into the Dubna and it in turn into the Volga. Because of the convenience of these rivers merchants make use of them, bringing their goods there even from the Caspian Sea by water and thence farther inland.

Byeloozero means the white lake; the town of Byelozersk and the castle on the lake come from the same name. The town is not upon the lake, as some have written, but is so girt about with marshes as to be deemed impregnable. Thus it is said that the grand-dukes preserve their treasure in a swamp in which they can take refuge in need. The town lies a hundred leagues from Moscow and the same from Novgorod, the shorter way through Uglitch in winter-time, the other through Yaroslavl. Both ways are so confused by forests, marshes and rivers as to make the leagues an under-reckoning. From these causes too it arises that no towns or boroughs or villages are to be found upon the way. The White Lake mentioned is said to be twelve leagues long and as much in breadth. Into it, they say, pour three hundred and sixty brooks or streams, out of it but one river, the Sheksna. This falls into the Volga fifteen leagues above Yaroslavl and four below Mologa. Such fish as turn into the Sheksna from the Volga are all the better for their stay in that river, and hence the anglers know how long the fish has been in the Volga as soon as it is caught. The inhabitants of this region speak their own tongue, although they can now all speak Russian. The longest day in these parts is said to be of nineteen hours. A reliable man told me that he had once been sent from Moscow to this place at the season when the leaves were falling from the trees, and had ridden as far as the Volga. As soon as he had crossed this river he completed his journey to Byelozersk by sledge upon the smooth winter track. Although the winter in these parts is longer, crops ripen quickly, so that the corn is cut here and in Moscow at about the same time.

A crossbow-shot away from the White Lake is another pool. It is said to yield brimstone, and the river which comes out of it brings this sulphur with it like a foam. But they have not been able to turn it to account.

Uglitch, castle and town upon the banks of the Volga, lies twenty-four leagues from Moscow, thirty from Yaroslavl and forty from Tver. Its castle stands upon the Volga facing south; the houses of the town are upon both shores.

Kholopigorod is a place where stood formerly a castle or town and to which fled the vassals of Novgorod who had taken their masters' wives. It is two leagues from Uglitch. Close by can be seen the stables of the former castle.

The River Mologa, flowing eighty leagues from its source in the Novgorod area, joins the Volga. At its mouth are a town and castle bearing the same name as the stream. Along the river bank two leagues from here is a church, that of Kholopigorod. Close by is a market greater than any other in Muscovy. It also sells debased gold and silver, or so it used to be said.

Pereyaslavl, with castle and town and facing between north and west, lies twenty-four leagues from Moscow and upon a lake in which can be caught the selgi fish mentioned in the description of the isle of Solovetski. The land here is fertile and the prince comes to hawk here after the crops are cut; close by is another lake from which salt is panned. The ducal party makes the round of Nizhniy Novgorod (Gorki), Kostroma, Yaroslavl and Uglitch. In these parts it is hard to reckon the leagues because of the many great forests and marshes. Also here there is a River Nyerl which rises in a lake and joins the Volga above Uglitch.

Rostov, with castle and town, is the seat of an archbishop and, together with Byelozersk and Murom, one of the oldest principalities save for Novgorod. The journey from Moscow is made to Pereyaslavl, then ten leagues beyond. Rostov lies upon a lake from which the River Kotorosl emerges to flow by Yaroslavl and into the Volga. The district is fertile, and abundant in fish and salt. This duchy was given to the Grand-duke's brothers many years ago, but lately they have been replaced by Grand-duke John.

The castle and town of Yaroslavl on the Volga, twelve leagues from Rostov upon the direct way from Moscow, have good lands, especially towards the Volga.

Vologda is the name of a duchy, a castle and a town. The river also has this name. Here live the bishops of Perm, but not as overlords. The town lies to the north-east; to reach it from Moscow you pass through Yaroslavl and then on another fifty leagues. It is forty from Byelozersk. The country is very marshy and thickly forested, so that even travellers can find no landmarks. The river flows north outside the town and into the Sukhona just as this leaves the Lake of Kubinskoe. The two rivers join eight leagues below the town of Vologda, the Sukhona keeping its name and flowing north-east. The town was previously under the rule of Novgorod; the castle is strong in order that the Grand-duke may keep there a portion of his treasure.

The Vaga is a river abounding in fish between Byelozersk and Vologda; it rises amid vast thick forests and bogs and joins the Dvina. The people there do not eat bread but fish and game. Black foxes are caught here and their pelts sold at high prices. This is the most convenient way into the Dvina territory.

The land of Ustyug (now Veliki Ustyug) bears the name of its town and castle and lies along the Sukhona. This is a hundred leagues from Vologda and a hundred and forty from Byelozersk. Previously the town was at the mouth of the River Yug, which flows from south to north. For convenience it was moved half a league upstream, retaining its name. The Russian *ustje* means river's mouth, thus Ustyug means the mouth of the Yug. This land too came under the rule of Novgorod. Here also bread is not used; there are abundant fish and game, as well as salt from the Dvina. The people have their own tongue. Not many sables are found here, and rarely good ones, but there are plenty of other furs and especially black fox.

The principality of Suzdal, together with town and castle of the same name, and seat of a bishop, lies between Rostov and Vladimir. At the time when the Russian grand-dukes had their seat at Vladimir Suzdal was one of the most notable duchies and a local capital. But as soon as the grand-dukes moved their seat to Moscow this principality fell to the second or younger of the Grand-duke's brothers, by whom Basilius Chuski and his nephew, who were still living in Moscow in our own time, were removed from the principality by the father of Basilius, John III. There is a noteworthy nuns' convent here, to which this Basilius (Vassili III) committed his first wife, Salomea. Among all the duchies of the grand-duke Ryazan comes first in fertility, and after it Yaroslavl, Rostov, Perejaslavl, Suzdal and Vladimir. (. . .)

Vyatka is a land stretching to the River Kama, some hundred and fifty leagues to the north-east by the shortest, but difficult, way from Moscow. It goes through Kostroma and Galitch, for between Galitch and Vyatka—apart from the many swamps and forests—live the roving and thieving Cheremissi tribes. For this reason travellers commonly go through Vologda and Ustyug, which is farther but more convenient and safer. Vyatka lies a hundred and twenty leagues from Ustyug and sixty from Kazan, the land and river having the same name. Along the latter are the following castles: Khlynov (now Kirov), Orlov and Slobodskoy. Orlov is four leagues below Khlynov, then it is six leagues westward to Slobodskoy. On the River Ryetshitsa, which runs from the east into the Vyatka between Khlynov and Orlov, is the castle of Kotyelnitsh, eight leagues from Khlynov. The land is boggy and unfertile and a no-man's-land of runagate vassals and miscreants. Game, fish, honey and squirrels abound. The Tatars have established themselves thoroughly here and prevail upon both sides of the River Vyatka down to its junction with the Kama. The Kama joins the Volga twelve leagues below Kazan. Skirting the water is the country of Siberia. The name of the league in which they reckon there is *chunkas*; it equals five versts and is thus about a German league.

Perm is an important and extensive territory which they speak of as Great Perm. It is two hundred and fifty leagues from Moscow, though some say three hundred, to the north-east. The town, also called Perm, (now Molotov) lies on the River Vishera, which joins the Kama ten leagues below.[1] It is almost unapproachable in summer by reason of the many marshes and streams, but can be reached in winter. The traveller wishing to reach it in summer must come along the Vologda, Ustyug and Vyshegda rivers and then embark downstream.[2] If one goes from Perm to Ustyug one must take boat upstream on the Vishera and then in sundry other rivers, carrying the boat several times from one stream to the next. This is why they reckon the distance to Ustyug at three hundred leagues.

Bread is rare in this land. They discharge their annual tribute to the Grand-duke in horses and skins. They speak their own tongue and have also their own writing, which a certain Bishop Stephen invented at a time when his wavering belief was re-affirmed. This Stephen was counted a saint in the time of Grand-duke Demetrius (Dimitri Donskoy), son of John (Ivan II). Once in the past these Permans flayed a bishop. Idolaters are still to be found in the forests, and Russian monks or hermits often go to them there and strive to turn them to the true faith, even unto this day. (. . .)

Siberia is a land which borders upon Perm and Vyatka. I have been unable to learn whether there are castles and towns within it. Here rises

[1] Herberstein seems to have got this wrong. Perm lies on the Kama about eight leagues below where the Vishera joins it. Tr.

[2] i.e. the water-borne traveller must make a long detour to the north. Tr.

the River Jaik (Ural) which runs into the sea called Caspian in Latin and Khvalinskoye in Russian. The country is exposed to the pillage of the Tatars and others, especially of the Tatar Shikhmamei. These people too have their own tongue. Here are to be found the finest and largest minivers or calabers. I saw some the first time I was in Moscow, but not since.

The Cheremissi are peoples living in the forests beyond Nizhniy Novgorod (now Gorki) and having their own especial language. They are of the Mohammedan faith and in obedience to the King of Kazan, although they have heretofore paid tribute to the Muscovites who wish to retain them as their vassals, which is why I mention them now. When I was on my second mission the Grand-duke had seized a large number of these Cheremissi, men and women, alleging that they were trying to secede from him, and had them brought to Moscow where I saw them. He distributed them towards the Lithuanian frontier and many withdrew later into Lithuania.

The inhabitants from the Vyatka and Vologda down to the River Kama and all around live without houses and are all, men and women, quick and nimble on their feet and masterly archers, the bow leaving their hands but rarely. They do not give food to their older children, who satisfy themselves from their own shooting. The women cut from the bark of trees something like the martyrs' painted crowns which they wear upon their heads in a hoop and covered with a piece of cloth. When I asked them, who passed so often through the shrubs and trees, how they managed with such lofty head-dresses, they replied: 'We pass through like the stag, who has much taller things upon his head.'

The Mordvins, another people who live below Nizhniy Novgorod along the southern shores of the Volga, resemble the Cheremissi in every way save that they dwell in houses. And now I must finish my account of the Muscovite lands.

Seven leagues up the Dnieper from Cherkassy is Kanev, and eighteen farther upstream is Kiev, the noble, ancient, former capital of Russia. What it was once like can still be seen in the remnants of buildings and in the marvellous hill cemeteries with their preserved corpses. All around there are abandoned convents and churches to behold.

From trustworthy persons I have learned that the girls here rarely remain chaste beyond the age of seven, but have not heard of any credible and reasonable cause. It is not forbidden to merchants to have their pleasure of them but it is to carry them off. And he who permits himself to carry one off and is caught loses both life and property.

III

THE PEOPLE

'They are a pitiable people, their lives and property the prey of the nobles, and soundly thrashed as well.'

'Their affection for their wives is indifferent, for they take them unseen and must put up with them.'

'They often stand and sing before their houses, clapping their hands so that they resound.'

I RANKS AND CLASSES

The title or word *Knyaz* was often to be heard. They have always used it, adding *veliki* to mean 'great' or 'grand' as in grand-prince or grand-duke for those who have more than one duchy under them. But those who have but one use the title Knyaz without addition.(. . .). Among the rest there is no special rank except for the *boyars*, who might be considered nobles in our country; the less important ones they called boyars' sons. *Boy* in Wendish means war, so that they might be called warriors.

The boyar or nobleman, however poor he is, deems it a disgrace to work. But when we or our servants cast away the skins of fruit such as apples, pears or melons they were not ashamed to pick them up and eat them, even onion peel. Frugal eaters, they go to extremes with drink. Their dissoluteness does not exasperate, but they are very arrogant in their penury. This is followed by pitiful servility. The doors in their houses are low and their thresholds high, so that when they enter them they must abase their little caps deeply and, in their long, tight robes, lift their feet up high. I explained to them the reasons for these motions: so that their necks should remain supple, and so that they should be in practice for mounting a horse. But the real reason is to keep the cold out of the rooms.

The servants of the wealthy have all been bought among their own or captured people. If they should have a freeman as a servant it is not seemly that he should ever leave his lord, and if he went away without his master's consent nobody would take him on. If one of the lords treats a good servant badly all the others are afraid of taking service with him and he can find no servants.

The peasants must serve their masters six days in the week; the seventh is their own. They are allotted a patch of ground with which they must be content and are a pitiable people, their lives and property the prey of the nobles, and soundly thrashed as well. They are called, as though abusively, 'Christian' and 'bogyman', for there are always two living together, one working for his master and the other for the house.

It is in the nature of these people that they should vaunt their bondage more than their freedom. Dying masters often liberate many of their bondsmen in their last dispositions. Few of these stay free, for they sell themselves. A father will sell his son in this manner. If the son frees himself by a service or in some other way the father may sell him a second and a third time. But after this the father has no further authority over him.

2 WIFE AND WEDLOCK

A man who sues for the hand of someone's daughter is despised. It is the father who chooses the suitor, saying to him: 'I approve of you and your activities and therefore offer you my daughter in marriage.' The young man replies: 'I will speak to my friends about it.' If both sides think well of it negotiations are concluded and the wedding-day named. If the bridegroom wishes to see his bride before the marriage the father says: 'Ask other people. They will tell you what she is like.' When the bridegroom is committed but the agreement not yet firm he may not see the bride before the wedding and its consummation. Dowries commonly take the form of horses, clothes, weapons, cattle, servants and such-like.

The wedding guests rarely if ever present money, but other gifts. The bridegroom takes careful note of the source of each present. After the wedding he looks over the presents to see what he intends to keep, sending it to the market for valuation. He returns all the others to where they came from with a word of thanks. But what he has kept he pays for within the year according to the valuation, or cancels the obligation with other gifts. If some man rates his gift more highly than the sum the bridegroom will pay or meet, the latter must accept the juryman's valuation. If the groom does not pay for a present within the year he must pay double, and if he has not had it valued by a juryman he must accept the owner's valuation. They deem it inadmissible to marry within the fourth degree of kinship, or that two brothers should wed two sisters. Nor may a man take to wife the sister of his brother-in-law. God-children may not marry their sponsors. A second marriage is tolerated but does not rank as highly as the first, for they do not regard it as true marriage. Unless there are important reasons for it a third marriage is not allowed, and a fourth is forbidden because they deem it unchristian. Although they like to conceal it, divorce is commonplace and bills of divorce are issued. The Grand-duke divorced the barren Salomea, whom he had had for twenty-one years, and compelled her to a convent. Some years ago a certain Knyaz Byelski absconded from Lithuania to Moscow and they would not allow his young wife to follow him, believing that he would return because of her. When he took legal advice the Metropolitan decreed: 'Because you have not brought it about that your wife cannot live with you I shall grant you the mercy of the law and separate you from her.' Upon which the man took a princess from Ryazan who gave him sons who were highly esteemed by the Grand-duke (and whom we also met). (. . .)

They do not speak of adultery nor pay regard to it, unless one party has harmed the other. Their affection for their wives is indifferent, for they take them unseen and must put up with them. It is curious that nobles and other respected persons, who spend much time on duty and in travel, often forsake their wives and practice other unnatural things.

No woman who walks in the street is deemed chaste or respectable. Thus wealthy or important people keep their women so shut up that no one can see or speak to them; they entrust them with nothing beyond sewing and spinning. The women conduct their domestic affairs by themselves with male servants. The quantity of fowls, birds and fish that the women have to slaughter puts them off their food. Wives of poorer men who have to slaughter something when their menfolk are away stand at the door with the hen, or such-like, and a knife; when a man passes they ask him to slay it. The women are rarely allowed to go to church, and much less often to visit friends, unless they have grown so old as to be beyond attention and suspicion.

A German artificer and gunsmith named Jordan, of Hall in the valley of the Inn, took a wife with whom he lived for many years. One day she asked: 'Why do you not love me?' He replied that he did. 'You give me no proof of it,' she went on. He asked what proof she was thinking of. 'You have never beaten me,' she said. He rejoined that he had never held blows to be evidence of love, but would not fail her in the matter. Soon after he gave her a sound thrashing. He told me himself that she had never been as affectionate as previously. Finally he struck her dead.

3 DAILY LIFE

Their normal clothing is of a single pattern: long, tight coats with narrow sleeves, almost like the Hungarians'. Down the front are buttons done up on the right, which distinguishes them from the Tatars who wear similar coats buttoned on the left. Their knee-boots are usually red, with small nails in the soles and some in the point in front; at the raised heels the boots have studs which serve as spurs. Their shirts all have high capes of various hues and usually fitted with gilded buttons, as many as their wearer can afford, or with pearls at the side to hold the cape together. I have written elsewhere that their girdles seemed strange to me at the time, but now one sees German and others presenting great bellies—although the Germans were reckoned massive and heavy without this.

I shall now tell how they receive each other in their houses. Each one has in the room or apartment in which he normally lives a sacred portrait, painted or cast, over his seat. As soon as he enters the room the guest looks round for the icons, bares his head and crosses himself thrice according to their custom. Only now does he say to his host: 'I wish you good health!' They take each other's hands and kiss. Each bows his head to the other, each keeps an eye on the other to see that he does not bow too slightly, for each of them wishes to appear the more polite: the bowing goes on ever longer and deeper.

They transact all their affairs with each other sitting and never do business as they walk; they often marvel at our habit of doing this. When matters have been settled the guest stands up, goes to the centre of the room, bares his head towards the icons and crosses himself. And uttering the very words with which he entered, he goes away. According to the identity of the guest his host accompanies him to the door of the room or as far as the staircase. If the status of the guest is even higher he is accompanied down the stairs to the landing. No junior or inferior person rides into the premises of his senior or superior, but dismounts in front of them. However unassuming the nobleman may be he rarely leaves his chair at home, in order to preserve the respect of others. Thus it is hard for poor folk to come to see him. If a noble wishes to visit another three or four houses away he rides, or his horse is led after him. But when it is smooth and icy in winter they go to court or church on foot, for the horses are not shod and it is dangerous to ride. Their cloaks and staffs are carried behind them by servants; when a noble goes afoot he takes the staff in his hand. Younger and lesser persons are not allowed the staff.

Women and their daughters are allowed to assemble in the meadows in summer. There a wheel is commonly rigged up in such a way that one or more who sit upon it are whirled round and round from the bottom to the top. Or they hang up a ropework in which one of them seesaws to and fro. These frolics often bring bad falls. Also they often stand and sing before their houses, clapping their hands so that they resound. They have no dancing.

The sturdy young lads commonly have some ground within the town where they gather on holidays. As the custom is, one of them gives a whistle, upon which they rush upon each other, striking and punching each other with fists, knees and feet in the face, throat, belly or genitals so that some are always carried off half dead. This takes place for the honour of holding the fort longest and also to harden them to blows with which, when given in earnest, they will be familiar.

IV

THE STATE

'All in the land call themselves their prince's kholopi, *or sold slaves.'*

'All those whom he (Vassili III) wants to employ at court, in war or in diplomacy must do so at their own expense.'

'The presence of so many people on such a day, summoned to the castle and herded into it, arises from two causes: so that foreigners may note the size of the crowd and the mightiness of its lord and also so that vassals may note the respect in which their master is held, being visited by such great potentates in the persons of their respected ambassadors.'

'They attack their enemies defiantly but do not persist long, behaving as might happen anywhere in our own lands when the feeling was: run, or we shall.'

I POSITION OF THE GRAND-DUKE

All in the land call themselves their prince's *kholopi*, or sold slaves.

The Grand-duke exercises his power over both clergy and laymen, both property and life. None of his councillors has ever dared to gainsay his lord's opinion. One and all agree that their lord's will is the will of God, hence what the prince does is divinely inspired. Thus they call their prince God's *klyuchnik* or key-bearer, in the sense of chamberlain, and only regard him as the fulfiller of God's purpose. So when someone pleads for a prisoner he will say: 'What God orders will take place without your plea.' And when one asks about something to which there is no proper answer, they say: 'God knows and the Grand-duke.' It is debatable whether such a people must have such oppressive rulers or whether the oppressive rulers have made the people so stupid.

Albeit he (Basilius III) has been unfortunate in war, yet his people called him successful. And when there remained not the half of his troops they dared to say they had not lost a man. He surpasses all other kings and princes in the power he has and uses over his own people; what his father began he completed. That is, he turned out the princes and others from all the fortresses, neither leaving nor entrusting any fortress to his brothers. He holds one and all in the same subjection.

Pskov was formerly called both Pskov and Obskov; it had a large territory and was a free city. But the Grand-duke John (Ivan III; in reality it was Basilius III) captured it in 1509 through the surrender of certain ecclesiastics. He carried off the bell which had hitherto served the purpose of calling the people together, and subjected them to perpetual servitude. The population was taken out and distributed elsewhere, and Muscovites installed in its place, a change which completely altered the standards of good manners and behaviour and kindness. Previously the inhabitants were honest, persevering quietly at their tasks and never overcharging: a bargain was made with a single word. Those still left in the town retain the habit of wearing their hair all over the head and not done up in a bun.

The third brother (John of Ryazan) arrived with the support of the Tatars, wrested the duchy from his mother and began to negotiate with the Grand-duke of Moscow so that he might reign independently like his forefathers. During these transactions it was proposed that he should make overtures to the Tatar King of Perekop, with whom the Grand-duke was then at war, for the hand of his daughter and he was therefore summoned to Moscow. Being apprehensive he put off this journey, but was persuaded by the representations of his counsellor Simon Crubin and set off. There he was detained under guard in honourable captivity. The Grand-duke evicted his mother, sending her to a nunnery and taking possession of the duchy. And in order that the populace of Pskov should not rise against him he distributed and intermingled them in other duchies. Thus came about the decline of this notable principality. When the Tatars were drawing near to the city of Moscow in 1521 the imprisoned Duke of Ryazan broke out and went to Lithuania, where he was living in exile at the time of our journey.

Kashira lies upon the banks of the Oka six leagues above Kalomna.

The town had previously its own lord. Basilius (Vassili III) was notified that this lord was plotting his death. The Grand-duke therefore invited him to a hunt. The worthy lord was persuaded to come armed to the Grand-duke. But he was not allowed to reach the prince's presence, for Michael, son of the prince's secretary George, took him into the little town of Serpukhov close by and commanded him to declare himself. The secretary brought him a cup, to be drunk to the Grand-duke's health according to custom. The lord soon grasped how matters lay, asked for a priest and accepted the cup. He died quickly. In this way the Grand-duke acquired Serpukhov too, lying some eight leagues from Kashira.

Among the other duchies that this same Basilius (Vassili III), son of John (Ivan III), brought under his rule was that of Severia. Two brothers had each a son. One of them was nicknamed Shemyatshich and held court at Novgorod Severski, the other at Starodub. At Putivl was another prince, Dimitri. Shemyatshich was a warlike man, feared even by his neighbours the Tatars, and wishing to be sole lord he drove his cousin Basilius out of Starodub. After this he attacked Dimitri with other wiles, giving the Grand-duke to suppose that the latter wished to secede from him. So the Grand-duke commanded Shemyatshich to seize Dimitri and bring him before him. Shemyatshich overtook him while hunting, having previously sent out horsemen in advance. When Dimitri fled homeward these revealed themselves and took him. So he was led prisoner to Moscow.

Because of this oppression and injustice the son of this Dimitri fled to the Tatars so that he might avenge his father, and had himself circumcised. Meanwhile Dimitri's son had fallen in love with a girl and, being unable to secure her in any other way, carried her off secretly against the wishes of her parents. His servants, circumcised like him, revealed this to the friends of the abducted girl, who lay in wait for him at night and shot both him and the wench. When the Grand-duke heard of this elopement he stiffened the father's captivity all the more. From this and the news of his son's end Dimitri died soon afterwards in 1519. Shemyatshich was the prime cause of it, as he had also been of the deaths of the lord of Kashira and his brother, who both expired in prison.

It often happens that the man who plots the downfall of others falls into the trap himself. This was the fate of Shemyatshich too. A similar charge was lodged against him and he was accused of seceding from the Grand-duke. He was summoned several times but refused to appear unless provided with a safe-conduct and an escort and guaranteed by the sworn oaths of the Grand-duke and the Metropolitan. Thus provided he came to Moscow on 18 April 1523. He was honourably received to begin with and given presents, but a few days later he was cast into prison and was still there during our visit.

The cause of his confinement was alleged to be letters he had written to the King of Poland offering to secede to him. He was said to have sent these letters to the governor of Kiev, who had opened them and forwarded them to the Grand-duke. Another cause put forward is more credible: that there remained in all the territory of the Grand-duke no single land with a fortress at its command save for Severia, and that the power of the Grand-duke would be all the firmer if this fell also. This may have been also the opinion of the jester who rode with them to meet Shemyatshich carrying a broom and spade, with which he frequently made a little heap upon the road and then cast it away with the shovel. When asked what he was doing he replied that Moscow had been fairly well tidied and swept, that there was only one pile of rubbish left and it was high time to clear it away.

Similarly the grand-duchy of Yaroslavl was entailed to the brothers of the Grand-duke, but they were likewise deposed; the *Knyazya* or princes who have inherited such duchies are still living. But the Grand-duke gives them some of the revenues, retaining the bulk of them for himself together with the title and most of the income.

2 GOVERNMENT, ADMINISTRATION AND JUSTICE

If ever they talk to us about Lithuania they speak mockingly of it, saying for example that when the king or grand-duke there dispatches a man upon an embassy or journey he replies that his wife is ill or his horses lame. 'Here this is not so,' they say with a smile, 'here it is: you will ride off and obey orders if you want to keep your head upon your body.'

The Grand-duke's senior councillor, treasurer and chancellor, a Greek known as little George, once held the same opinion (that the Russian church is not entirely orthodox), and was for this reason stripped of all his offices and disgraced. Nevertheless the Grand-duke could scarcely get on without him, for he was learned and experienced in many things. So he was taken back into favour but given other duties. Once the Grand-duke had need of him when he was ill and sent for him; when the Greek reached the foot of the stairs the prince ordered several of his stateliest councillors to carry him and the sledge in which he sat up into his room. The Greek resisted being carried comfortably upstairs and the Grand-duke grew very angry: the visitor must be brought up notwithstanding. After he had given his counsel he was carried down again. On my second mission to this prince little George was no longer to be seen.

There are three nephews of the Grand-duke. One of them, Basilius, brought us from our inn to the Grand-duke and back again. The second, Simeon Fyodorovitch Kurba, called Kurbski after one of his estates, is an elderly man who has borne himself soberly and frugally since his youth. For many years he has eaten no meat, and fish only on Sunday, Thursday and Saturday; on Mondays, Wednesdays and Fridays in Lent he does not eat at all. The Grand-duke sent him off through Great Perm against the Jugrians to conquer vast territories. He made much of the journey on foot because of the heavy snow; when this had gone he completed it by skiff upon the brooks. The third, Knyaz Ivan Posadnik, who was sent by the Grand-duke to Emperor Charles in Spain, came upon his homeward journey to Grand-duke Ferdinand, later Holy Roman Emperor, my most gracious lord. I accompanied Ivan back to his master. He had become so impoverished that he had to borrow clothes and the little cap they call *kalpak* for the journey. Whoever wrote that this man could provide his lord in any crisis with thirty thousand mounted men from his own territories was much mistaken.

Every two or three years the Grand-duke has a list made of his nobles' children so that he may learn how many servants and horses are attached to each one sent to or grown up in these domains. He pays the boyars an annuity, as already mentioned, but those who are wealthy must serve without pay. He grants them little rest, for he is commonly at war. (. . .) After the yearly distribution (of posts) he summons certain of them to serve at court in Moscow.

Whoever he (Vassili III) employs at his court, in war or upon a diplomatic mission, must bear the cost himself save for the boyars' sons, or poor noblemen. To these he pays six *gulden* every three years, payment being made in the third year. Those who have an agreed salary of twelve gulden, however, must set off with their horses upon any errand at any time at their own expense. The more distinguished, employed in embassies and other larger affairs, are given not money but offices, villages or some other form of clearly defined income, usually for eighteen months unless there is some special bounty or other cause for extending them by some months, provided always that the normal interest and income from these sources comes to no less for the Grand-duke. These people may retain the fines and suchlike they grind out of the poor, and he who neglects his own interests in this period cannot count after two trienniums upon the prospect of a third. In the meantime he must fulfil all services and commands at his own expense.

When ambassadors to foreign emperors and monarchs are honoured with gold chains, drinking vessels or other presents, all pass into the keeping of the prince with the intimation: 'Such things do not beseem you, I will do you other favours instead.' (. . .) Knyaz Ivan Posadnik Yaroslavski and Simeon Trophimov, the secretary, were both sent to Spain to Emperor Charles V. There they were presented and rewarded with dignified chains and Spanish double gulden, and later the Emperor's brother, my master Archduke Ferdinand, gave them silver-gilt goblets and other articles of gold and silver as well as Austrian coins of gold and silver. They travelled with Count Nogarola and me to Moscow. As soon as they arrived they were obliged to lay everything before the Grand-duke, who confiscated all save a few of the lesser Spanish and Austrian coins. I questioned one of them about it but he prevaricated. The other said: 'The Grand-duke wanted to see it all.' When I repeated my questions later more than once the former ceased to visit me, being afraid that he must either tell a lie or fall into anxiety and danger with the truth. But the courtiers did not deny it, saying: 'What does it matter as long as they receive other favours in return?'

Basilius Tretyak Dalmatov was a pleasing secretary to the Grand-duke. He commanded him to carry out a mission to Emperor Maximilian. But when Dalmatov asked for his travel expenses, the prince having twice ordered him to set off, he was on the third occasion arrested and taken to the White Sea, remaining a prisoner for the rest of his life. His possessions, trinkets and money were taken by the Grand-duke, including three thousand gold pieces of which his brothers and heirs received not one.

The prince has post-horses in every locality within his domains. When a man travels with the post he is brought several horses so that he may choose one that he likes. When I was travelling with the post from Novgorod during my first mission the post-boys, whom they call *yamshtshik*, brought out at every station twice as many horses as I and my servants needed. From these each took the one he wanted.

He who travels on the prince's orders and has a horse fall under him—even he who is not under grand-ducal orders but travels with the post—may take and ride anybody's nag to the next posting station (called a *yam*). Should there be nobody there he rides to the nearest houses and takes whatever horse he finds or fancies. On entering the post-yard each removes his saddle and bridle and lays them upon the new horse, all the horses a man rides having the same saddle and bridle. If a horse has to be abandoned by the wayside the post-boys will find it and also pay for the replacement taken in its stead. I learned that the prince pays six *dengen* for a horse ridden from one yam to the next, twenty or five-and-twenty versts. When my horses could not budge, my servant rode from Novgorod to Moscow, a hundred and twenty leagues, reckoning at five versts to the league, in seventy-two hours.

As soon as one has arrived at the post and removed saddle and bridle it is the business of the ostlers to drive the beasts to a meadow or patch of snow, according to the season, wipe them down, allow them to roll a few moments, and then put them in a stable. They receive no fodder until they are as cool as though they were leaving the stable for the first time. Then they are given hay and driven to the water, receiving as much hay as they desire. The common horses are fed but once and at night, so that the men are on duty night and day. But the animals are led or driven to water twice a day.

Highwaymen are treated with the strictest justice. When captured their heels are cut off or crushed and they are left lying a day or two until these swell, and it is thus that they are carried about. In their suffering they will answer any questions. When one of them is found guilty he is hanged; they have no other form of execution unless the culprit is guilty of grave crimes. I have seen men hanging whose feet had fallen off or been eaten by the wolves and seen the wolves eating them, so close to the ground are they strung up.

Common thieves are rarely punished with death, nor even murderers, unless guilty of highway robbery. A man who catches a thief at work and kills him is not punished provided that he brings the body before the magistrates and describes what took place.

Few authorities have the power to take life. None of the vassals may use torture. Many criminals are taken off to Moscow and other sizable towns. Courts concerned with these matters are held only in winter, the summer being taken up with military affairs. Here follows an extract from the Ordinances and Laws of Grand-duke John (Ivan III), son of Basilius, of the year 7006 (1497):

When the accused is fined one rouble he shall pay two *altyn* to the judge and eight dengen to the clerk. If the parties come to terms before reaching the place of contest they pay the judge and notary as if a trial had taken place. If they reach the place of contest indicated by the *okolnik* and the *nedyelshchik* and come to terms there, they pay the judge as above, fifty dengen to the okolnik and the same to the nedyelshchik, and four altyn and one *denge* to the clerk. But if the contest takes place the loser shall pay the judge whatever he demands, giving the okilnik one *poltina* and his armour, fifty dengen to the clerk and to the nedyelshchik one poltina and four altyn. But when there is a duel over a fire, the death of a friend, robbery or theft and the complainant wins he may take what he likes from the loser; the okolnik receives one poltina and the loser's armour, the clerk fifty dengen, the nedyelshchik one poltina, and the *veston*, the man who brings the contestants together according to established rules, four altyn.[1] And whatever the loser still possesses shall be sold and given to the judges and he shall receive corporal punishment in proportion to his misdeeds.

Those who kill their masters, betray castles or towns, despoil churches, those who take something into the house of another and then say it has been stolen from them—they call these *podmetshik*—fire-raisers and notorious criminals are punished with death. A man caught in his first theft, other than a church robber, may not be executed but is publicly punished, that is to say flogged, and fined by the court. If he is caught a second time and has nothing with which to pay the accuser and the judge, he is to be executed. And if a man is convicted of theft and has nothing wherewith to pay complainant and judge he is to be flogged and handed over to the complainant. If a person is accused of theft and an honest man testifies on oath that he has been previously convicted of theft or has compounded such an offence, he shall be put to death without further judicial decision and his property be dealt with as above. If a man of low estate and poor reputation is accused of theft he shall be brought before the bench; if not convicted he shall be released on bail pending further inquiry.

Village magistrates order one of the parties to pay a sum of money and forward their opinion to the official judges. When these recognize

[1] The relative values of the Muscovite coins occurring on this page are given on p. 82.

it as just and fair one altyn of every rouble falls to the judge and four dengen to the clerk.

Whoever wishes to accuse a person of theft, murder or robbery comes to Moscow and requests that the person be summoned. A nedyelshchik is attached to him, who names a day and brings him to Moscow. Usually the accused denies the charge. When the complainant produces witnesses both he and the defendant are asked if they accept their evidence. Normally they reply: 'The witnesses shall be heard according to justice and custom.' If they testify against the accused he may object to them on personal grounds or to their evidence, saying: 'I desire to keep my oath and, commending myself to divine justice, request combat and to know the meeting-place.' This is consented to according to their law and custom.

Each may nominate a substitute for the combat and use whatever weapon he chooses, but not guns or bows. Often they wear a couple of long cuirasses, one on top of the other, armour and whatever they fancy. Usually they take a pike, an axe and a kind of knuckle-duster through which the hand can be put and nevertheless be used for any purpose: above and below the hand at each end it has sharp spikes.

Their first weapon is the pike. For some years now the Muscovites have constantly lost their contests with foreigners. Recently a young Lithuanian of the age of sixteen did battle with a Muscovite who had previously won a score of victories. The Lithuanian struck him down. This angered the Grand-duke and he summoned the young man. When he saw him he spat in his face and wrote an order that foreigners should not fight Muscovites from then on. The latter encumber themselves with weapons, whilst the foreigners use their heads and skill. They usually go about together and have taught their duellists to keep their distance, for the Muscovites are strong of arm and hand. Stones had been set out for the young Lithuanian in several places and at first he pretended to give ground to the *batyr* (this is their name for a worthy man) and had recourse to the stones, heaving them one after the other and thus winning the struggle. Each contestant usually has many supporters who have no mail, but carry sticks. When one side thinks that its champion is being unfairly treated the partisans often come to blows, which it is merry to watch for they scuffle only with fists and cudgels.

The testimony of a nobleman carries far more weight than that of the common people, who rarely have an attorney or advocate and must state their case themselves. And, awesome as the prince may be, a verdict can none the less be bought and this is no secret. We were told that a respectable alderman accepted profits and advantages from both parties and gave judgment for the one that gave the more. The matter being taken before the prince, the alderman made no denial but added: 'This one is rich and honourable and thus the more worthy of belief than the poor man.' Although the prince suspended the judgment he nevertheless laughed and let the alderman go free. Perhaps the great poverty is one cause of such avarice and injustice, and because the prince knows this he winks at it. Poor folk have no recourse to the prince, only to the aldermen and that with difficulty.

The okolnik is no more than a magistrate nominated by the prince; the chief councillor, a permanent member of the prince's household, has this status also. The nedyelshchiks have the duties of summoning to court and catching criminals and imprisoning them; they are of the boyar class.

This same Vladimir [1] also subjected to the ecclesiastical court all abbots, priests, deacons and the entire class of churchmen, monks, nuns and the women baking the bread used for the sacrament. They call the bread *proskura* and the women needed to bake it, so old that they have lost their bloom, are called *proskurniza*. Further, priests' wives and children, physicians, widows, midwives, those who have had a revelation from a saint, those liberated by the last wish of the dying, and all servants of the convents and hospitals who make the monks' clothing. Whatever quarrels arise among these persons must be judged and dealt with by the bishop. But those arising between them and a layman are heard in the common court.

The bishops also deal with the separation of married people and those who cohabit. The bishops' jurisdiction extends also to cases in which a wife is disobedient to her husband, a person is taken in adultery or prostitution, marriage within the tables of affinity, or evil designs upon the spouse. Furthermore petitioners in cases of witchcraft, poisoning or heresy; uncouth behaviour by a son to his parents or family; unnatural vice; spoliation of tombs or removal of portions of images and crucifixes for purposes of magic; introduction of dogs, birds or other unclean animals into church or the eating of them there. In addition the bishops have to determine and impose standards in all things. No one should be surprised that repugnant matters are mentioned in this account, for in many places in the course of time this

[1] The Great or Holy, monarch at Kiev, 980–1015.

or that custom has changed or prevailed and become distorted by considerations of gain or self-advantage.

Summer travel

3 TREATMENT OF FOREIGN EMBASSIES

When an ambassador approaches the borders of Muscovy he sends a messenger with a letter or verbal request to the steward or governor of the nearest town, giving the names of the envoy and his master. Presently there are inquiries about the status and rank of the ambassador and the identity of those with him: they wish to know the names of all, including servants, and also their fathers'. According to the significance of the lord sending the embassy and the rank and reputation of the ambassador, a party is made up and sent to the frontier to receive the visitors. The governor also sends post-haste to the Grand-duke in Moscow all the details mentioned above.

Whoever has been charged by the governor to meet the embassy sends someone to the ambassador in his turn, thus demonstrating that a personage of importance has been dispatched to the frontier to receive him, with the message that he will await the latter at such and such a place. Instead of titles they use the word 'great', referring to their prince and others not as Highness, High and Well Born, His Honour and so on, but compressing this into the single word 'great'.

When the two parties meet, perhaps in deep snow, the governor's emissary takes the road with his sledge and traces a new track, so that the embassy may travel along it when the time comes, the ambassador waiting humbly on the road. Then the governor's man comes up and indicates that the embassy may dismount from its sledges or horses. And he will see the ambassador standing before he dismounts himself, thinking thereby to maintain his lord's prestige. If the ambassador alleges fatigue or other reasons for transacting matters in the sledge or on horseback, they will reply: 'It is not seemly to speak or to hear my lord's words other than standing up.'

Western traveller. Compare with illustration on page 75

On my first mission I rode with the post from Novgorod. Someone was sent to meet me as I drew near to the city of Moscow. The interpreter Istoma came forward and called upon me to dismount. I excused myself as being very tired; if it could not be otherwise, I said, the other man should be the first to get down. After spending some time over such pompous talk I wanted to make an end of it, and shook my foot out of the stirrup. Upon this the other envoy dismounted at once, whilst I climbed slowly from the saddle. I too wished to preserve reverence for my master among these wild people. When both the visiting envoy and the governor's are on foot upon the boundary, the latter bares his head and says: 'The governor and captain of N., in the name of the great lord Basilius, king and master of all Russia and its grand-dukes (here followed a list of the remoter grand-duchies) has ordered me to inform you that when he heard you were sent by such a lord to our great lord, he dispatched us to meet you —they repeat the titles of the Grand-duke and the governor every time—and commanded us to inquire how healthily you travelled (this is their standard welcome: how healthily did you travel?), ordering us to accompany you. Only after this does he offer the envoy his hand. From now on he bares his head only if the envoy has done so first. Then he asks as though on his own behalf: 'How healthily did you travel?' With a gesture he bids one remount, saying: 'Mount and ride.' Himself he stands still on the road, so that the envoy's party must pass close by him. He remains at the rear, not to do honour to the ambassador but as though to close the road to anyone who might wish to join the party or drop out of it.

On the journey they ask again for the envoy's name and that of each member of the party down to the lowest servant, and the names of all their fathers, what lands and tongues each one may know and of what rank he is, whether he is in the service of another lord as well, whether any of the party is the ambassador's friend and whether he has been in these parts before. This is all written down and conveyed quickly to the Grand-duke. Presently comes a man saying he has been sent by the governor to provide for all the party's needs along the road, and then the clerk attached to him. They provide everything required by man or beast.

Dubrovno is the name of a castle and small town in Lithuania lying upon the Dnieper. From there we rode eight leagues to the border of Muscovy. We spent that night in the open in the chill of the snow, close to a brook which surged up when the snow melted. Then we repaired the bridge, thinking to pursue our way soon after midnight and get as far as Smolensk, which would have been only twelve leagues. After about one German league their emissary came to meet us and received us as I have described. Barely half a league farther we were shown our bivouac. Next day we again covered about two leagues and slept in the open, though this time the Russian envoy entertained us and looked after us well. This was the eve of Palm Sunday.

When we observed on Palm Sunday that we were again to be kept in the open in the snow we ordered our couriers not to dismount before Smolensk. When they had gone two leagues with our laden sledges they were nevertheless shown our prospective camping-ground, and were prevented from riding on. We arrived and wished to continue; they deterred us with much supplication, and we consented to breakfast there. On this day Count Nogarola entertained the Muscovite couriers Knyaz Ivan Posadnik Yaroslavski and Simeon Trophimov, the secretary, who had been to the Holy Roman Emperor in Spain and were travelling with us.

I could readily guess why they kept us so long upon the way. It was because we had announced ourselves late and they were therefore awaiting instructions from Moscow about how to delay us and whether we were to be admitted into Smolensk or stopped outside it. For this reason I set out for Smolensk after our meal. There was a general stampede, the envoy and his camp being upon a mound in front of us with a small brook running in between. His people informed him of our revolt. Soon some of them came riding after us, bidding us remain with entreaties and sometimes threats. One of them said: 'Sigmund, what are you about, riding about a foreign lord's land at your pleasure?' I answered that I was not accustomed to take shelter in the open among wild animals, but to dwell among other people and under a roof. 'Your master's envoys could travel about my lord's domains by day or night at will, and were taken to towns and markets and good inns. I require the same here. I know too that this treatment does not accord with your master's orders and I know of no urgent reason why you delay us so long upon the road.'

They tried to take us off the road into the houses of some village, saying that night approached and we should not be admitted to the town so late. Disregarding these arguments we set forth for Smolensk. We lodged close below the town, having the ice hacked from the stable doors so that our horses could go in. In the morning they led us over the Dnieper and put us in two good houses facing the town, and there we rested that day and night. The governor sent us malmsey, Greek wine, three sorts of mead, and some bread and other food. Here we had to wait ten days for the Grand-duke's answer. Then two of them came from Moscow, the streams being high in flood. These two were *pristavs*, as they call them, men sent to help us on our way to Moscow. Well dressed, they came to us in our quarters and we awaited the moment for baring our heads. When they were explaining their business and uttered the name of their prince we duly removed our hats, upon which they bared their heads for the first time.

Just as we were much delayed upon the way to Smolensk, so we had to wait long in that town. To put us in good humour the two men came and announced departure the next morning. We arrayed ourselves and waited for them; they came just before vespers and said again that we should travel next day. We waited that day also, everything in readiness, but it came to nothing. We were kept waiting two whole days in this state of preparation. On the third day too we waited until noon, taking no food lest we should lose an hour if they came.

On this day they fixed upon so long a journey that our supplies and baggage could not keep up. The rivers and streams were rising and to be crossed only with much labour and care. A bridge that we repaired or made would be carried away in half an hour. This was why, on the second day's journey from Smolensk, Count Leonhard von Nogarola was nearly drowned. I had gone deep into the water and come to a bridge which was afloat; I was standing on it and giving directions about the passage of our saddles and gear by this means—for the horses are swum across—and the Count's horse stood boldly by the Muscovites', who had stopped there as though they had no part in the business. In the bustle the Count's horse slipped his hind legs into the depth of the stream, for it was not possible to tell where the bank lay.

The horse was bold and jerked itself out; the Count fell backwards from his saddle and, fortunately, hung from his stirrups, emerging from the depths with the horse. He freed himself in the shallows, lying upon his back with his Spanish cloak covering his face and unable to help himself. The two Muscovites stopped close to him, and neither stirred to help. They were wearing their *yapantchen*, as they call their cloaks, for it was raining slightly. My two cousins, Herr Ruprecht and Herr Gunther, brothers of Freiherr zu Herberstein etc., came to his aid, Gunther nearly falling into the river himself. I rated the two Muscovites for not having helped the Count, and they replied: 'It is seemly that one man should do work, but not the next one.' After which the Count had to strip and put on dry clothes.

From this bridge we came to another large stream on the same day. The peasants sent in advance had made a raft there and laid across a rope of willow to which the raft was attached. Upon this we made a slow and perilous crossing. Next came another bridge, approached and left through long stretches of water. I saw some cross who could barely struggle up on to it, and night was beginning to fall. On this occasion I did not desire to go over, for our food and other wagons could not follow.

I went into a cottage and asked the housewife for bread, oats and other necessities, which she gave willingly for cash. When this was told to the Russians attached to me he forbade the woman to give me more. When I learned of this I commanded him through his deputy to take thought and hand over the food promptly or at least allow me to provide for my own necessities, failing which I should give him a drubbing. I am familiar with these people, who take and sell something provided and then pretend they have provided it themselves, and here they were trying to stop me from buying with my own money.

I added that if he acted in any other way I should carry him to Moscow with me in bonds and other dreadful threats, knowing the usage of these lands. He came to me soon after, exceptionally uncovering his head. I carried out none of my threats but I crushed his arrogance.

After this we came to the junction of the rivers Vop and Dnieper. Here we laid our baggage in the ships and sent them upstream. After we had crossed the Dnieper and come to a convent where we spent the night our horses had next day to swim thrice over small streams within a single half-league. A monk conveyed the two of us by boat through a flooded forest to where we joined our horses. This monk then took the rest of our party, who had not swum the horses across, by instalments together with the saddles and other things; and so we set off again on horseback.

On 26 April, as we were approaching Moscow and within half a league of it, the envoy Simeon, who came from Spain and had accompanied us from Vienna, rode up sweating and at top speed to announce that his lord was sending important people to receive us, mentioning them by name. He added that it would be seemly to listen to his master's words standing, and therefore to dismount. After this we shook hands and chatted. Among other things I asked him why he was sweating. He replied loudly: 'Sigmund, it is one thing to serve your master and another to serve mine.'

As we rode forward we saw a long string of people in a field. As we drew near they dismounted and we did the same. When we met, the chief among them spoke: 'The great lord Basilius, sole king and master of all the Russians', etc. giving all the titles, 'has learned of the arrival of you both, ambassadors of his brother Charles, elected Emperor of the Holy Roman Empire and supreme monarch, and of his brother Ferdinand. He has sent us, his councillors, with instructions to inquire of you after the health of his brother Charles, elected Emperor of the Holy Roman Empire, etc.' Then the same about Ferdinand. We answered in the customary manner: 'By the grace of God each of us has left his lord in good health.'

A second said: 'Count Leonhard, the great lord Basilius—with full titles—has commanded me to meet you, conduct you to your lodgings and provide you with necessaries.' The third one was saying precisely the same to me, and all with heads bared. Then the first one resumed: 'The great lord Basilius,' etc. with full titles, 'has ordered me to ascertain from you, Count Leonhard, how healthily you travelled.' Upon which a second said the same to me. We answered according to their custom: 'May God grant that the Grand-duke is in good health. By the grace of God and the indulgence of the Grand-duke we have travelled healthily.'

Then one of them spoke again: 'The great lord Basilius etc. has sent you, Count Leonhard, this palfrey and saddle and a second horse from his stable.' A second said the same to me, and we both expressed our thanks appropriately. Only now did they give us their hands, all asking each of us how healthily we had travelled. They also said that it would be seemly if we did honour to their lord by mounting these horses, which we did.

Soon we came to the River Moskva and crossed it, although we sent all our baggage over first. On the bank close by was a convent, and then a fine lawn reaching to the town. Soon a great concourse of people was to be seen and they escorted us to our lodgings, two sound wooden houses in the local style standing opposite each other. They were empty inasmuch as there was nobody within, only tables and benches, and no hides hanging at the windows. All this was made good.

The persons now attached to us, who had accompanied us from Smolensk, presented themselves to their new masters saying they had orders to provide us with all necessaries and would bring us food and all we needed each day. They brought to us our clerks and begged us to tell them of anything we lacked, they visited us daily to ask if there was anything we required.

There is a general ordinance laying down for Germans, Lithuanians, Livonians or Tatars who come upon a mission how much bread, meat, fish, salt, pepper, onions, oats, hay, litter, brandy and other drink shall be allotted each day, reckoned from the number of persons and horses; the same also with wood for kitchen and stoves. There is also an ordinance for those making journeys. They gave enough of everything according to their own usages; for my part I was well sated. Five kinds of drink were brought daily in a little pony-cart, three of mead and two of beer. Fresh fish was not provided as it is not the general custom. I therefore sent to the market a few times to buy it with my own money. When they learned of this they protested, saying that I brought shame upon their master. After this they provided fresh fish on every fast day.

I spoke to them about providing beds for some of my friends and other noblemen who were with me. 'It is not our custom,' said one of the Muscovites, 'to supply beds.' I said that this was not what I was asking, but that they should not be put out if I bought them. The next day they came back saying they had discussed the matter with the councillors. 'They have bidden us tell you that you are not to spend your money. Since our ambassadors have reported that they and their followers have been given beds in your countries we shall provide them for your people too.'

We established ourselves and rested for two days. Then we asked our pristavs when the Grand-duke would grant us audience. They answered: 'Whenever you desire we will inform the councillors.' We desired it there and then. We were at once informed of the time, although it was altered by one day. In the morning the pristav arrives and says: 'The Grand-duke's councillors have commanded me to announce to you that you are summoned by our lord tomorrow.' The interpreters always come too for such announcements. In the late afternoon of the same day the interpreter comes back and says: 'Make ready, for tomorrow you go before the Prince.' On the following morning the interpreter returns, reminding us as before: 'Today you will come into the lord's presence in about half an hour.' The pristavs go to each of us with the same news: 'Great nobles have been summoned because of you and it would be best if you were together in one house.' Upon which I go across to the Imperials'. Soon the pristav returns with the announcement: 'Great nobles and those in the Grand-duke's highest favour have been summoned because of you. Keep at hand, and you will be taken before the Prince.'

One of the great men was Knyaz Basilius Yaroslavski, a close friend of the Grand-duke's. Then there were many of the boyars or, as we would say, nobles. The pristavs were badgering us all the time to do honour to these great folk and go forward to meet them. We replied that we had had some experience in the matter. When the visitors rode up to Count Nogarola's house the pristavs urged us forward to meet them, in the intention that our master would thereby be acknowledging theirs as the greater. We took both motives as reasons to delay until the visitors reached the staircase, when we went forward. We asked them if they would care to withdraw to the upper rooms to rest. But the very first said: 'The great lord Basilius etc. has commanded that you should appear before him.'

We mounted forthwith and were taken all round the castle before reaching the right gate. So many people were standing there that we could scarcely get through. Such is their custom when foreign envoys are brought before the prince. Nobles and servants living close to the town are summoned, loafing round markets and squares is stopped and the order given that the common people are to assemble before the castle, to which they are driven. As we went into the castle the burgesses were standing before us, but towards the churches and the Grand-duke's residence were all manner of soldiers. By St Michael's Church are the stairs leading up to the Grand-duke's quarters. They will not allow anyone to ride deliberately up to the staircase, saying that this is reserved for the prince. Half way up the stairs we are met by more of the prince's envoys, who clasp our hands and embrace us. At the top of the stairs stood the *boyarski dyeti*, or lesser nobles, and when we were beyond the staircase there were other councillors, who greeted us with handshakes and kisses. Farther on towards the closed apartments came yet others to meet us; those who had welcomed us at the staircase came among us and those who had accompanied us from our quarters had to give way. The second and third groups did the same, so that we were always accompanied by those who had last greeted us, the others following behind.

We entered the apartments in the company of those who had joined us last. In the first of them people were dressed in velvet or silk ornamented with gold; from these come the men chosen at any moment for important posts. We went into a second room, coming after this into the presence-chamber. Of all those we passed not one stirred or gave any sign of recognition, whether he knew us or not, and it was the same later on: even though I knew one of them and he me he would show no sign of recognition. When I bowed towards them and greeted them, none acknowledged or gave any sign: they stood or sat like logs.

The men in gold and silk and costly apparel who received and presented us, as well as those sitting with the Grand-duke, are all clothed by the Treasury and each must contribute to the cost of cleaning the garments. The presence of so many people on such a day, summoned to the castle and herded into it, arises from two causes: so that foreigners may note the size of the crowd and the mightiness of its lord and also so that vassals may note the respect in which their master is held, being visited by such great potentates in the persons of their respected ambassadors.

When we went into the room where the Grand-duke was and made obeisance there were many other princes and persons sitting round. They all stood up, albeit they and the Grand-duke remained seated when his brothers appeared. Then one of the chief councillors, who may perhaps have been a Lord in Waiting, came towards us and said:

'Great Lord, King and Master of all the Russians, Count Leonhard strikes or bows his head before you.' Then a second time: 'Count Leonhard strikes or bows his head, thanking Your Majesty for his grace and favour'. Then the same with Sigmund. The first part, with its bow, is the token of homage, the rest refers to the hospitality and the present of the horses. 'Striking the brow' is the common phrase for doing honour or expressing thanks; they use it when making petitions and in many other senses. A man seeking or giving thanks for a bounty from a greater person bows his head and body so deeply that his hand touches the ground. If the bounty proves difficult or if a favour is sought from the Grand-duke himself the man prostrates himself upon his hands and touches or strikes the ground with his head. Hence comes the term 'striking the brow'.

The Grand-duke's throne is higher by a hand's length than the tabouret. His head was uncovered most of the time. Above him on the wall he always has an icon of God or an angel or saint; on the seat on the right is his kalpak, on the left his sceptre, called a *posokh*, and a bowl with two small jugs and towel on top of them. He is said to maintain that when he offers his hand to one of the Roman faith it is defiled; thus as soon as the envoy has moved away he washes his hands and cleanses them. In front of him was a very low bench, covered with a carpet, upon which the envoys sat.

When the speeches of reverence and thanks are done the Prince says to the envoy 'Rise' or 'Advance', pointing to a seat close to the bench. As soon as the greeting is over and the name of the Emperor uttered the Grand-duke stands up, steps off the footstool and says: 'And how is the health of our brother Charles, elected Roman Emperor and supreme monarch?' When he hears the reply: 'Good, by the grace of God', he resumes his seat and hears the rest of the greeting. Then he bids the envoy to be seated and gives him a moment's respite. After this he calls the interpreter, whispering to him to say to the envoy what is to be said in public and keep the rest for another time. Then the envoy stands and explains his errand, the interpreter not accepting more than two or three words at a time. After this the Prince singles us out, saying to each: 'Give me your hand,' and adding: 'How healthily did you travel?' To which we reply: 'Great lord, may God grant that you long live in health. By the grace of God and your indulgence I am in good health.' Then he commands us to be seated. Before we sit down in front of the Prince we bow to the councillors and others standing in our honour.

When embassies from lands such as Lithuania, Sweden, Livonia etc. arrive it is the custom that they bring gifts to the Prince. These are handed over in public after their first reception—not only by the ambassadors, but by the more eminent members of their entourage as well. How they are presented follows later. After a mission has delivered its message one of the senior councillors goes before the Prince —it was the one who received us three times and presented us—accompanied by those bearing gifts. The councillor says: 'Great lord, N. strikes his brow and offers *pominki*,' and he then enumerates the presents. Near by stands a secretary who writes down the name of the donor and what he brings. When we had delivered our message those behind us said, 'Pominki', reminding us to hand over our offerings. Our people told them that such was not our custom. Previously we used to make such gifts thrice, presenting them to many and at much cost, but this has been changed as is explained later in reference to the dismissal of the Lithuanians.

After being ceremonially greeted we were commanded to sit down, the Grand-duke inviting each of us by name with the words: 'Leonhard, will you take food with us?' On my first mission the Prince used his normal phrase and asked if I would take bread and salt with him. Then he summoned the pristavs attached to us and whispered something to them. They came over to us and, through the interpreters, bade us rise and go into another room to which some of the councillors had been sent. We presented to them the others of our party.

Meanwhile the boards were being laid and the dishes arranged after which we were led to table. Together with his brothers and most of the councillors the Grand-duke was sitting at a long table, the former rising as we entered. Opposite the Prince's table was one set out for us, the Prince showing us himself where we were to sit. Before we did so we bowed to him and the standing councillors, according to their usage, and thanked them for welcoming us thus.

I sat next to Count Nogarola, and after me was a space large enough for two covers. Then came our friends and the others of our escort. Opposite each of us sat a Muscovite, usually one of those who had brought us to court from our lodging. On the Prince's right sat his brother at an arm's length, on the left the other brother similarly. After him came an empty place, then a long array of senior councillors and officials. Two other tables were also occupied, making a ring of tables round the room with a gap for entrance into it by the door. In the middle was a sideboard richly laden with gold and silver. At the two remaining tables were various scions of the Tatar kings who had been baptized and now served the Grand-duke, and others he had invited; among these were master-gunners and such persons. At our table and no doubt at the others too, save for that of the Prince and his brothers, it was so arranged that there were always four guests to each dish. Vessels holding pepper, vinegar and salt were on the board throughout the meal. On my first journey Czar Peter was there too, a Tatar monarch who had been baptized. He had married the Grand-duke's sister and sat on the right of his elder brother during the banquet.

When we had taken our seats the stewards filed in through the door and stood before the Prince around the sideboard in their rich clothes. None made any obeisance to him; they walked with heads up as though they did not see him. After this the Grand-duke called his butler or cup-bearer, taking three slices of bread which had been specially cut and laid on top of a pile and giving them into his hand with the words: 'Give this to Count Leonhard, envoy of our brother, elected Roman Emperor and supreme monarch.' This butler summoned the interpreter on duty before the table and said: 'Leonhard, the great lord Basilius, King and Lord of all the Russians and Grand-duke, does you the favour of sending bread from his own table.' Then he went a second time and said the same to me. These utterances are spoken loudly by the butler and interpreter. When such gifts and speeches were directed at us we stood up. As soon as we did so all those sitting near us stood up too, only the Prince and his brothers remaining seated. After receiving the bread we bowed our thanks to the Grand-duke, then to the councillors nearest him, after which we bowed to the other side and in front of us. It is their custom that the Prince marks his favour by sending bread from his own table; if he sends salt this means affection, and it is reckoned a greater honour to receive salt. This fine white bread is baked in the shape of a horse-collar, and I reckon that those who commonly enjoy it have earned it by heavy toil and hard service.

Presently the stewards are sent to fetch the dishes. Meanwhile brandy is served, usually drunk before the meal. When there is meat they always bring in roast swans first, two or three of them being placed before the Grand-duke, who prods them with a knife to find out which is the most tender while the remaining stewards stand holding their dishes and their swans. Then the Prince orders the removal of the one selected, upon which they all move over to the door. Here stands the serving-table where the swans are carved, always four wings or four legs to a dish and then the rest as they think fit. Now the stewards bring out the dishes once more, placing four or five—for they are not large—before the Grand-duke and others before his brothers and the privy councillors, then the ambassador and finally the rest.

Meanwhile the Prince seeks out the tender cuts, calling a servant to take one on a dish to one of his brothers or privy councillors, or after them an ambassador. He to whom such is sent stands up and the others stand up to mark his honour; he thanks the Prince and the rest with a bow. All is dispatched with much ceremony. When the Prince bids his servant deliver something he cuts off a piece or takes a crumb of bread and gives it him to eat; he also carves something for the steward and gives it him for sampling.

All these tokens of favour sent hither and thither mean so much standing up that one is positively fatigued, especially when the next table is so close that one cannot stand up straight. On my first mission I noted that the Grand-duke's brothers were not highly esteemed, and since they did not stand up for me, an ambassador, I did not stand up for them. The man opposite addressed me and bade me, since the Grand-duke's brother was upstanding, to rise also. I chose the moment to speak to somebody as though not understanding what was taking place, then I finally looked about and raised myself a little for a few moments. When those opposite noticed this they tittered among themselves, and I asked them why they laughed. When none of them would make reply I said gravely: 'I pay fitting respect to him who does honour to my lord, but not to him who fails to do so.' And when the Prince was showing favour to some of the younger and less important and sent them something from his table, this was why I stood up before them although informed that I need not do so on account of their youth; none the less I stood up. The Prince saw that my neighbours were laughing and that I had been talking with them on the matter, and asked one of them what it was all about. No doubt he explained, and the Prince laughed too.

When we began to eat the swans they sprinkled them with pepper and poured vinegar and salt upon them. They have also soured milk and salted cucumbers, preserved for a year at least, standing upon the tables in various places. The other dishes are brought forward in the same way, although they are not taken out again like the swans. A variety of drink was set before us, malmsey, Greek wine and several sorts of mead. Often the Prince would request a drink, taste it and then summon the ambassador to come over to him, saying: 'Leonhard, you come from a great lord to a great lord on great affairs and have made a great journey. May you prosper now that you have felt my favour and looked me in the eyes. Drink and drain it, eat your fill, so that you can rest and return to your master.' The same was said to me. And on the same occasion the Prince asked me if I had clipped my beard, expressed in the single word: 'Bril?'. I said I had, using also this word. 'You followed my example,' he added, meaning he had done the same, unprecedented in a prince in such a country, for he had, when he took his second wife, had his beard clipped off.

All vessels upon the sideboard and the service from which we had eaten, drunk and taken pepper, vinegar and salt were of gold, as could be told from the weight apart from other evidence. Both previously and afterwards I was a guest of the Grand-duke when the sideboard and tables were laden with silver. Four servants stood by the sideboard each holding a vessel from which the Prince was wont to drink. At table he bore himself humanly enough, often addressing us, exhorting us to eat and drink, asking us questions. The first time I was at the Grand-duke's his servants and stewards were dressed almost like the assistant priests of our great churches, but not the second, when they wore something like a tabard which they call *terlik*, well garnished with pearls from the Prince's treasury.

Banquets last very long; some kept me until after one o'clock in the morning. All business is done before the meal. When transactions are afoot they eat nothing until night. In compensation they often spend the whole of one or several days in gluttony and drinking. At the end of a banquet the Prince tells the ambassadors when to leave; those who brought them are soon at hand to take them to their lodging. Here the members of the escort seat themselves and say they have orders to stay with us and cheer us up. They bring a cart with silver vessels and one or two with drink—the carts are small. With them arrive secretaries and other respected persons to help to fill the envoys' skins. For making people tipsy is here an honour and sign of esteem; the man who is not put under the table holds himself ill respected. The Muscovites are indeed masters at talking to others and persuading them to drink. If all else fails one of them stands up and proposes the health of the Grand-duke, upon which all present must not fail to drink and drain the cup. After this they try to provoke toasts to the health of the Emperor and others. There is much ceremony about this drinking. The man proposing the toast stands in the middle of the room, his head bared, states what he desires for the Grand-duke or other lord—happiness, victory, health—and wishes that as much blood may remain in the veins of his enemies as drink in his cup. When he has emptied it he reverses the cup upon his head and wishes the lord good health. Or he will take up a prominent position, have several cups filled, and distribute them with the motive for the toast. Then each goes into the middle of the room, drains his cup and claps it on his head. I disliked and still dislike tippling and could only get out of this by pretending to be drunk or saying I was too sleepy to go on and had had my fill.

When I took leave of the Grand-duke at the end of my first mission he was standing after the meal—for it is their custom to invite envoys to dine upon arrival and departure—by the table at which he had sat. He ordered a cup and said: 'Sigmund, we will drain this in honour of our brother Maximilian, elected Roman Emperor and supreme monarch; you shall drain it too and all the others afterwards in token of our affection for our brother Maximilian etc., and you shall tell him what you have seen.' Then he offered me the cup, saying: 'Drink it to the health of our brother Maximilian etc.', naming his titles. After which he gave a cup to each of the others and addressed each in the same manner. Taking the cups we stepped back, keeping our heads inclined towards the Grand-duke, and drained them. After such a toast he would call me to him, give me his hand and say: 'Go now.' Upon which I withdrew to the lodging.

It is also the Prince's habit to invite ambassadors to course or hunt beyond the town. Just outside it are many patches of woodland where hares can lie, and there is severe punishment for anyone who traps them. Here they multiply profusely and many are lured into gardens and houses. If the Grand-duke wishes to take a jaunt with envoys or others all the hares to be found are brought into the same woods and, together with those from other coverts, driven into one or two groups and surrounded with nets.

Thereupon many huntsmen come forth, each leading two dogs and wearing parti-coloured clothing. When they loose the hounds in the woods they go forward together with loud shouting such as will dislodge any beast; in front are swift dogs on leash, which they call *kurta*. When we drew near to the Prince in the field we were required to dismount and go up to him. He gave us his hand and said through the interpreter: 'We set forth for our pleasure and have summoned you to share in it and have enjoyment yourselves. Mount and follow!'

He was wearing a white kalpak, but one with collars, and where the collars were cut were gold ornaments on both sides in the shape of feathers which fluttered up and down as he rode. His coat was a terlik, like a tabard, ornamented with gold thread. Two knives hung at his belt, as is their custom, and a third for striking or protection. In the small of his back was a weapon which they call a *kisten* or *basalyk* in Polish. It is of wood, two or three spans long, and to it is riveted a strap of a couple of spans from the end of which hangs an angular or rounded piece of iron or copper. This is how it is commonly fashioned; the Prince's was of better materials.

On one side of the Grand-duke rode the exiled King of Kazan, Schig-Ali, next to him on the left were two young noblemen. One carried an ivory battle-axe like those upon the Hungarian gulden, the other carried a Hungarian mace, also of ivory, which the Hungarians call *buzogany* and the Russians *shestopero*, meaning of six feathers. The Tatar had the bows and arrows of his sort and a sabre at his side.

Some three hundred horses had taken the field. The Prince often called to us to move this way or that, usually nearer to himself. As we drew near to the meet he told us that it was the custom, when he felt so inclined, that he and his friends took the hounds to the meet on leash, and that we should do this. He therefore allotted to each of us two hounds and two huntsmen. We thanked him and said that notable persons led hounds to the meet in our country too. His explanation was that persons of standing in Russia do not touch a dog with bare hands because it is deemed an unclean animal. Hundreds of huntsmen stood about on foot, half wearing black and the others yellow, and the horses formed a cordon so that the hares should not escape.

Then the order was given that no one was to give chase in front of King Schig-Ali and us. The Prince himself cried out the command to cast off. The chief huntsman rode off into the crowd, who began to shout and to give chase. Leaders and other hounds had been distributed systematically. When a hare showed itself he was not only pursued but hunted from the side and in front. When he was caught there arose the cry of 'Ho! Ho!', as though some large wild beast had been stricken down. The hares no longer coming forth for some time, the Grand-duke himself cried 'Hui! Hui!' to those in the thicket with the captive hares, signifying that they should be loosed. But they were sullen and unwilling to run; they leapt and bounded and were soon seized by the hounds. The dog that seized most was deemed to have done best. If one of our hounds reached one first the Prince was pleased and praised him. After such coursing they brought the hares together, of which there were about three hundred.

Horses from the Prince's stables were also out but not as fine ones as I had seen before; they were better bred than the Turkish, and called *argamaks*. There were many splendid gerfalcons, which they call *kretshet*. Though wild they are not as terrible as reported by him who wrote that when a hawk or sparrow-hawk or other bird of prey catches sight of one of these he falls down dead from fear. But it is established that when hawks, sparrow-hawks and common falcons are in flight and one of them espies a gerfalcon, they all dive down and cease flying, even if pursuing other birds. With gerfalcons they catch swans, cranes and such-like great birds. Several reliable persons have told us that when gerfalcons are taken young from their nests and several placed together in baskets or mews, none will harm its neighbours and they treat each other with seemliness. When food is brought they allow the older to take it first: if Nature has truly endowed them thus they come very close to Reason. And however cruel they may be to other birds they do not give offence to each other. They cleanse themselves not in water, like other birds, but always in sand. They long only for cold or coolness, and by nature they prefer standing upon ice or rock.

After the hunting or coursing the Grand-duke repaired to a tower of wood standing half a German league from the town of Moscow. Several tents had been pitched close by: a large square one for the Prince in which many could harbour, another for King Schig-Ali, the third for us ambassadors and various others providing all that the Prince might need. Each of us was conducted to his tent to change clothing. When the Grand-duke was dressed he sent for us. He sat in an ivory chair with arms, with the King upon his right. We were shown to seats facing him, like envoys in audience. Beyond King Schig-Ali sat the privy councillors and on the left the younger princes and others favoured by the Prince.

As we were seated there they brought us sweetmeats of coriander, aniseed and almond in dishes, then the peeled nuts we call walnuts, then blanched almonds and right large sugar-cones. These were borne by servants, who knelt before the Prince and then came to the King and us. After this they fetched drinks, the Prince manifesting his favour and esteem as though at table. On my previous mission the Grand-duke had dined here too with the consecrated bread, which they term Our Lady's bread, hanging above him; they speak of this and enjoy it with great respect, hanging it in their houses and venerating it. The tent had stirred so that the bread fell down into the grass. The Grand-duke was alarmed and all the others stood up in fear. A priest was summoned to pick it from the grass.

After these creature comforts the Prince sent for us and we were once more escorted to our lodging, having ridden across the River Moskva in both directions. The large slabs of this floating bridge are tied to each other and reach from shore to shore. If several horses come together upon one portion it sinks so that they are in the water. When they move on it floats on the surface again, the one portion holding up the next so that none is fully submerged.

The Grand-duke has another pastime for some of the envoys. Wild bears are kept penned up and one is set free among several poor peasants armed with forks of wood; they have to catch him and often some injury is done. When one of them is injured he runs to the Prince saying: 'Lord, have pity on me!' The Prince answers: 'I will take pity on you,' gives him a coat and some corn and heals him thus.

A worthy citizen of Cracow, Michael Meydl or Spies by name, pleaded with me most earnestly despite all my excuses to take the young son of one of the citizens, Erasmus Bethmann, upon my journey. He was well set up, by no means ignorant and spoke passably well, but such a drinker that he lost his wits over the wine. I was thus compelled to have him put in irons. One day he asked for the money that his friends had given me for his needs. With this he won over three Muscovites and my cartwright, who was a Pole, set off southward towards the town of Azov and swam across the great water of the Oka. As soon as the Grand-duke learned that he had ridden off the post-boys everywhere were sent in pursuit. Those who crossed the Oka and the Don explained the affair to the men building works against the invasion of the Tatars, and these men sought and found the party's hoofmarks.

As they followed these they encountered a peasant from whom they learned that the five fugitives had constrained him to show them the way to Azov, he escaping in the night. Upon this they followed the hoofmarks and one night descried the fugitives by their fire and about to go to rest after eating their meal and turning their horses out to graze. The pursuers crawled forward upon their bellies and drove off the fugitives' horses. My cartwright woke up and sought to bring them back. As he passed among the men lying hidden in the grass they leapt upon him and threatened him with death if he made a sound. Upon which he was bound and laid in the grass. They drove off the horses farther still. A second one awoke meanwhile, saw what was afoot and came after them, then a third, each of whom was treated like the cartwright. Then the pursuers turned to the others. Erasmus had plenty of spirit, and stood defending himself with drawn sabre. When they asked him what he could do all by himself, he called out to the cartwright. Learning that this man upon whom he counted had been taken, he cast away his sabre saying he wished neither to be free nor to live without the others. They could have reached Azov in two more days.

I came under suspicion among the Muscovites, as though this man had set off on my orders or with my knowledge. When the prisoners had been brought to Mozhaisk I asked that the two of them might again be put into my hands, offering to pay the expenses involved. The answer came back that it would be unseemly to hand over one who came to them for instruction in the true Christian faith. The cartwright they sent back without difficulties.

Hearing that it might help Erasmus and perhaps free him from further complications, I told my pristav or attaché that people abroad would speak ill of the Grand-duke if they heard that he seized people in the foreign embassies. To prevent this, it seemed to me, the Grand-duke should summon Erasmus and his advisers before us all; if he declared publicly in front of us that he desired to remain in Muscovy because of his faith, we could all take note of this and no reproach could fall upon the Prince. This took place. I spoke openly to Erasmus about the matter; he agreed and I added: 'If you had made your bed better you would lie in greater comfort.'

Count Nogarola had with him a Pole who spoke to Erasmus privately and learned that he feared punishment from me; he asked if he might travel with the Count wherever he should go. The Count asked me if I had any objection, but I was pleased with this solution for I feared that the friends of Erasmus might have thought that I had possibly treated him unfairly on account of his money. The Grand-duke permitted Erasmus to travel with the Count, and thus we came to depart.

When the missions came to their end we were again bidden to a banquet. Presentations were made before it began. The Count and I were each given a dress of gold, lined with sable, with wide sleeves. The coat was wide too, which is not their fashion. These we had to put on and then go before the Prince. When we entered the councillor, whom we would regard as a chamberlain in my country, said loudly: 'Great Lord, Count Leonhard beats his brow before you', referring to the homage, and then a second time: 'Great Lord, Leonhard strikes his head', indicating his thanks for the favours shown. Then he repeating this, naming me, after which we were allowed to sit. The Prince said: 'Leonhard and Sigmund, you have witnessed what we have done at the instance of our beloved brother Charles, elected Roman Emperor and supreme monarch, and of our brother Ferdinand. You, Leonhard, are to tell our brother of this and you, Sigmund, his brother.' At table the Prince conducted himself towards us as we have already told and finally we drank his health as has also been described. In addition to the mantles of gold and sable the Grand-duke gave each of us eighty sable pelts, three hundred ermine and fifteen hundred miniver or squirrel skins. On my previous journey he gave me in addition to these presents a sledge with a large white bearskin on it, as well as a good white blanket which covered the sledge, and a fine great chestnut horse to draw it. Further he gave me many pieces of fish which had been dried or smoked in the air alone and without fumes or salt and came from a large fish they call byeluga: it is very long and without bones like the great sturgeon. He also gave me osetr and *sterlet*, species which are I think the same as Dück and sturgeon.

How ambassadors are received at the frontier and taken to Moscow and lodged, and how they are taken back to the frontier, I have already described. After the two of us were dispatched to Moscow by Emperor Charles and his brother Grand-duke Ferdinand to conclude peace or an armistice between the King of Poland and the Prince—a papal envoy, the titular Bishop of Skara, was also present—an armistice was achieved. The attendant ceremonies I shall now describe.

When we presented our petitions to treat for peace we received the rejoinder: 'If the King desires to treat with us for peace let him send his envoys here, as is the custom, and we will consent to a peace according to our situation.' We therefore dispatched envoys to the King in Danzig; Count Nogarola sent Gunther, Freiherr zu Herberstein, and I Hans Wuechrer. They were made knights in Danzig.

The King nominated the lords Peter Kiska, voivod of Plock, and Michael Bohush, his treasurer in Lithuania. As they approached, the Grand-duke of Moscow set off for Mozhaisk, ostensibly to hunt but really to prevent the Lithuanians, with all their horses and merchants, from coming into Moscow. We were members of his party. The

Lithuanian ambassadors arrived and had audience, handing over their pominki or presents according to custom.

We transacted our business there. Before it was concluded the Grand-duke sent back to the Lithuanian envoys and their followers all the presents they had brought, together with a gift from himself, in order to give the impression that they would leave without achieving their object and thereby frighten them into offering better terms. The Lithuanians were much upset, and asked for my advice. I gave it, recommending them to do no such thing: we should certainly learn beforehand if the Russians intended to dismiss them and should then have cause to request further negotiations. Nor was it the Muscovite's intention to reject the armistice, which we concluded despite his wiles.

When the armistice had been accepted and set in writing we were summoned to court and brought into a chamber where we were joined by the Lithuanian envoys of the King of Poland and after them the Grand-duke's councillors, with whom we had been negotiating the truce. They addressed the Lithuanians, saying: 'Upon the instances of these great princes our great lord has consented to discuss eternal peace with Sigismund, your King. Making no conditions for the time being the Grand-duke has hearkened to the intercession made to him and agreed to an armistice. He has summoned you to his presence so that it may be drawn up and put into effect.'

In their hands the councillors held the letters which the Grand-duke wished to send to the King, completed and with a small red seal hanging down. On the one side of it was the figure of a naked man upon a horse without saddle, and holding a spear with which he struck a dragon at the horse's hoofs; upon the other was an eagle with two crowned heads. The councillors had also a duplicate letter which the King of Poland, as Grand-duke of Lithuania, was to return. It bore the codicil: 'We, Peter Kiska, Voivod of Plock, Captain of Drohiczyn, and Michael Bohush Bohovitinovich, Treasurer of the Grand-duchy of Lithuania, Captain of Tslovin and Kamenets, ambassadors of the King of Poland and Grand-duke of Lithuania, acknowledge and kiss the cross in his name and have pledged our King to confirm this document by kissing the cross, in witness of which we have sealed it with our seals.'

When all this had taken place we all went together before the Prince. Presently we were shown to seats and the Grand-duke began to speak: 'Hans Franz, Count Leonhard and Sigmund, you have begged us on behalf of Pope Clement VII and in the names of our brother Charles, elected Roman Emperor and supreme monarch, and his brother Ferdinand to enter upon an everlasting peace with King Sigismund of Poland, which neither of us could obtain on any terms. You have therefore prayed us to accept an armistice. This we have done out of the love we bear your Princes. And because we deal fairly with the King,'—meaning that he was ready to confirm with oath or kissing of the cross—'we have made these transactions in your presence in order that you may inform your lords that you were present at the drawing up and confirmation of the armistice, and that we have entered upon it for their sakes,' etc.

Then he called his councillor Michael Georg, whose office is akin to that of Lord Chamberlain with our princes, and bade him take down the golden crucifix hanging above the Grand-duke by a thread of silk. The councillor took the towel lying by the water-jugs in the bowl with great reverence, grasped the crucifix and held it up in his right hand. One of the chief secretaries held out the two letters prepared so that the documents the envoys were about to accept could be seen and read. Upon them the Prince laid his right hand, holding the crucifix. He then stood up and addressed the Lithuanian ambassadors at length in the following terms: he had not rejected the peace with King Sigismund urged by the envoys of the great lords whom they saw before them, although acceptable conditions might be put forward from other quarters. Though it had not been possible to conclude a permanent peace he had accepted the armistice at the instances of the envoys. The provisions of the letters—he pointed to them—he would adhere to as long as God listed and he would guarantee this to his brother, King Sigismund of Poland, but he desired the King to return the identical letter and certify it a true copy in the presence of his ambassadors. 'Meanwhile you will pledge yourselves by all that is honourable that your King will set about this task and complete it,' sending the Grand-duke a letter in these terms through the Muscovite envoy.

Then the Grand-duke gazed upon the crucifix, crossed himself thrice after their custom, touching with three fingers his head and bosom, the right and then the left shoulder, bowing before the crucifix with the right hand hanging down, then stepping closer to the cross and moving his lips as though in prayer. Then he wiped his mouth upon the towel, spat forth and kissed the crucifix, touching it with his head and then each eye, and moved back and crossed himself and bowed his head as before. When this was done he bade the Lithuanians come forward and do the same. One of the Lithuanian envoys, Bohush, of the Orthodox faith, read the undertaking agreed upon and written down and Peter, a Roman Catholic, spoke after him, the Grand-duke's interpreter translating their words into Latin. After these readings,

Mounted Muscovite noblemen, showing Tatar influence. Quilted clothing, bow, side-arms, saddlery, bridles—even the manner of dressing the horses' tails—all are of a style that could not be matched anywhere in Herberstein's Europe, and all adopted from the Asiatic nomads who had ruled Russia in the Middle Ages

repetitions and translations the two Lithuanian ambassadors stepped forward and kissed the crucifix. Whilst they were reading and plighting themselves the Grand-duke was standing below the step with us and he asked me if I understood Russian. I replied that I understood some of it but not all.

Next the Prince seated himself and spoke: 'You have seen that we have given our pledge to our brother Sigismund, King of Poland, upon the special pleas of Clement, Charles and Ferdinand. Tell to your lords, you, Hans Franz, to the Pope, you, Count Leonhard, to Charles, and you, Sigmund, to Ferdinand, that we have done this for their sakes and so that Christian blood shall not be shed by our wars.' Such speeches are made at great length and always with titles in full. We returned thanks for his hearkening unto our masters and said that we would carry out his orders diligently.

Hereupon he summoned two of his councillors and secretaries and presented them to the Lithuanians as the men ordered to attend their king as envoys. Then he sent for drink. Not only did he himself offer a cup to us ambassadors and our noblemen and retainers but to all the others too, saying to the Lithuanians: 'Of what we have just done and what you have been told by our councillors you must inform our brother, King Sigismund.' Then he stood up and spoke: 'You, Peter, and you, Bohush, will convey our respects to our brother Sigismund, King of Poland and Grand-duke of Lithuania.' Upon which he bowed his head very slightly and sat down, calling each of them to him, offering them and their nobles his hand and saying: 'Go now', which was their dismissal.

4 THE ARMY

(The Grand-duke) leaves them [1] little rest. He is usually at war with the Livonians, Lithuanians, Swedes or Tatars, and even when there is no open war he keeps a force of 20,000 men guarding the frontiers against the sudden inroads of the Tatars.

Their horses are small, usually geldings, close-haired, unshod and with a simple bit. They ride with short stirrups, as though they wanted to lift their knees above the saddle. Saddles are also small and made so that the rider can turn right round to either side to allow of shooting with the bow. They cannot stand the shock of a lance. They use spurs little, but the lash commonly; it hangs upon the little finger of the right hand. When the bow or sabre is to be grasped—the proportion of riders with sabres is small—they drop the lash and it hangs from the finger.

Bows and arrows are their common weapons. They carry also a

[1] i.e. the boyars' sons in his service, or lesser aristocracy.

mace about two spans long to which is fixed a stout strap with a knob of copper or iron at its end, sometimes with a horn shaft sewn up in leather; the strap is about a span and a half long. With this arm they

Muscovite arms, equipment and saddlery

reckon to give heavy blows. They call it kisten in their tongue; in Polish it is basalyk. Only the wealthy carry sabres. A long curved knife, stronger in the back than a bread-knife and with a haft projecting but little from the sheath, hangs on their right with other knives and is used like a dagger at close quarters. Reins are long and so fashioned at the end that a man may grip them with the fingers and hold them fast in any emergency, like the lash. In this manner they can hold in their hands at one time bridle-rein, whip, bow, arrows and sword and make use of each as required. Those who are somewhat wealthier have armour rather like our cuirasses; the few helms to be seen are all pot-bellied or pointed. Others have habits thickly quilted with wool

Muscovite archer in quilted clothing with led horse

which will stop a normal arrow. Their spears are like lances. Their horses do not carry their heads well and are scraggy, but they work hard.

In their campaigns they make no use yet of artillery nor foot-soldiers, their single tactic being to attack or flee in haste. None the less, when the Tatar king from the Crimea had wrested the realm of Kazan from the Muscovites and installed there his grandson, coming within two leagues of Moscow upon his way homeward, Basilius (Vassili III) had encamped his army in the next year along the Oka and had a piece of field ordnance and a few infantry with his horsemen. He desired only to show his power and to wipe away the disgrace of having lain hidden some days in a hayrick—or else he feared that the Tatar would return. At the time that we were there he may have had fifteen hundred foot, Lithuanians and other foreigners. He had cannonaded Smolensk, casting the pieces before the walls and breaking them up afterwards; he carried the remnants away.

They attack their enemies defiantly but do not persist long, behaving as might happen anywhere in our own lands when the feeling was: run, or we shall. Towns and castles are rarely won by force but by persistent siege and by treachery. Smolensk was beleaguered with many guns brought from Moscow, but to no purpose. So they bombarded and set fire to the castle of Kazan; the men watched it burning and being rebuilt but none set foot in it. Although the Grand-duke had German and Italian gunsmiths and artificers, the Muscovites learned none of their skill, nor have they any notion of which piece to use for battles in the field and which for the attack or defence of walls. This was recently evident when the Tatars were in the land and threatening to make so bold as to attack the castle of Moscow. One of the castellans summoned the German gunsmith and said: 'Good Niklas, take the great gun down to the gate.' It was an ancient piece of iron, like a mortar, which had lain there for years; a man might squat upon the little powder-bag lying in its mouth and even sit up there. Master Niklas laughed. The castellan grew angry and asked why he mocked him. 'In three days,' said Master Niklas, 'I could not bring it down and make it ready, and even if it were brought there the gate would fall down at the first shot.'

In war too each nation differs from the next. As soon as the Muscovite betakes himself to flight he makes full use of it; he does not surrender or ask quarter, accepting blows but fleeing as long as he is able. Whereas the Tatar, though just unhorsed and lying sore wounded, strikes and bites and claws to the last breath. But the Turk, seeing that there is no hope, pleads with outstretched hands saying: 'Lord, bind but do not destroy an honest man.'

When the Muscovites make camp they take a broad ground on which the more considerable put up their shelters and tents. The others make a sort of canopy of rods with their yapanche, or cloaks, under which they store their arms, saddles and the like, sleeping there also. They leave their horses to graze unattended.

Many may wonder how they live with such little reward or maintenance. It is fitting to point out that when one of them sets forth with half a dozen horses only one of these is bearing his requirements.

First comes millet in a bag about two spans long, then a piece of pork, then salt, also in a bag. If he is rich he will have a bag of pepper and a kettle. Each has his axe at the back of the belt, and also his tinder-box. He makes no inroad upon his food as long as he can come by fruit, root vegetables, onions, garlic or game and fish. When all these fail he makes a fire and sets a kettle of water on it. He shakes in a spoonful of millet and some salt, and this satisfies both master and men—who of course get smaller portions. If the knight desires better victuals he adds a crumb of pork to season the whole, and this crumb is for him alone. This is what was told me of those of the middle station. The rich do better in every way. The captains and officers sometimes bid the poorer to their board; when one of them has had a good meal there, they say, he fasts for two days after.

When they go forth against the enemy their comfort lies in their number and they go no nearer to him than a bowshot. They strive at all cost to outflank him and fall upon him from the rear.

They make use of many trumpeters, and when they all start blowing in their own fashion it is strange to hear. They play too upon something like a shawm, which they call *surna*. Those who blow the surna do not desist for an hour or more, when they pause for breath. It is said that they can draw breath through the nose if they have filled their cheeks with it first in order to maintain the tone.

V

THE MUSCOVITE ECONOMY

'It is said that the stalks of grain commonly bear two or three ears and that the corn is so thick that it is hard to ride through, the quail not being able to fly forth because of its density.'

'The trade of the country is universally done by barter, goods and wares being rarely paid for with gold or silver but with other wares.'

I AGRICULTURE AND CRAFTS

The Grand-duchy of this name (Moscow) is in itself not especially important or large nor especially fertile, for a trifle too much drought or rain readily harms the sandy soil. And because of the boundless cold crops often fail to ripen properly. (. . .) On the other hand it often happens that there is excessive heat, as in 1525. Almost all the corn was parched and prices mounted so that what was bought before for three dengen now cost twenty or thirty.

The region has not been cultivated for very long, as the many stumps of trees show. They have what can be got from the plough, all else must be fetched from elsewhere. They have no cherries nor Mediterranean nuts, only hazel nuts. Their other tree fruit, such as there is, is not attractive. Melons they cultivate with zeal. They throw up the soil, as though from a plough, and sprinkle it with dung; then they lay more earth to the thickness of a span, take a dish and press out a hollow. In the midst of this they set the seed. If it turn cold the dung will help; if it is very hot they poke holes through the manure in several places so that air may pass in and save the seed or pips from stifling.

The district round Ryazan is held to be the most fertile of them all.

It is said that the stalks of grain commonly bear two or three ears and that the corn is so thick that it is hard to ride through, the quail not being able to fly forth because of its density. Honey, fish, poultry and game are abundant, fruit better or more appetizing than in Moscow.

The country along the Tanais (Don) is renowned for the quantity and quality of its fish, its air, herbs, plants, tree and other fruit, as though it were a planted garden. Game is so abundant and easy to come by that travellers need only salt and fire to support them.

Day labourers are paid one and a half dengen, or about four and a half Vienna pfennige. Foremen receive two dengen a day; they work badly enough unless they are soundly beaten. With servants it is as I told earlier of the wife: they think their master does not love them if they go unthrashed.

2 MONEY, TRADE AND COMMERCE

Their coins are not round but oblong, some of them cut with many corners. The one called the muscovite is known everywhere as a denge. It carries more than one relief, the oldest being that with a rose on one side and a horseman on the other. Other coins have inscriptions on each side. Six dengen make one altyn, twenty go to a *grivna*, hundred to a poltina, two hundred to a rouble. Later they struck half dengen, of which four hundred make one rouble.

Coins minted at Tver also have inscriptions on both sides, their values being like the muscovite. Novgorod coins have on one side a figure seated upon a throne, and someone bowing before it, and an inscription on the other; they equal two Moscow dengen. The grivna of Novgorod is worth fourteen dengen and its rouble two hundred and twenty-two. The coin minted at Pleskau bears on one side an ox's head with a crown and an inscription on the other. Here is a copper coin too, called *polan*; sixty of these equal a Moscow denge.

They mint no gold pieces, for they have no gold in the land but what is brought in—the occasional Hungarian or Rhenish gulden. The common rate for a Hungarian gulden was a hundred dengen, but it often changes. As soon as it is known in the market that there is a buyer with gold in his pocket they lower its value, but when someone requires gold they raise it. The coins of Riga are also in use, because of its nearness; their rouble is worth two of Moscow's.

The Moscow coinage was sound and contained little alloy, but they have now begun to counterfeit it and nobody is punished for this. Usually any goldsmith may mint. To him who brings in some of the local unrefined silver they give an equal weight of coins, naming as their charge a small silver coin which is paid in addition to the silver. Some writers have said that there is not much silver there and that the Prince has forbidden it to be sent abroad. Certainly they have no silver mines, but much silver comes into the country and it is accepted.

There is no need to forbid its going abroad, for barter is the universal means of trade: goods and other things are rarely paid for with gold or silver, but with other goods. No merchant trades with the intention of gaining silver or gold money; he means to carry back goods. They say themselves that it is not much over a hundred years since the small coins and money minted locally came into use. Previously they cast long strips of silver without any marks, and worth a rouble, but I could not find any of them. At Galitsh there was a mint too, but a small one and its coins have disappeared. Before coinage came in, they say, small transactions were settled with snouts and ears of miniver or, as some call them, squirrel: they themselves call them *byelka*.

He who brings goods to Moscow must show them to the customs men at once. They value them as they examine, and no one may buy them until they have been shown to the Grand-duke in case he desires to purchase, and the merchant cannot strike a bargain. Merchants are often long delayed in this manner. Nor are all merchants permitted to come to Moscow with their wares: of the Christians only the Lithuanians and Poles. The others, such as Germans, Danes, Swedes, Livonians and Hanseatics, have their offices and warehouses at Novgorod, where they keep their factors throughout the year. But when the market is held at Kholopigorod there come many Germans, Muscovites, Tatars and other distant peoples, Swedes and wild Lapps and all kinds of people from the northern Baltic. In such parts silver and coins have little esteem and gold none, save with the great merchants who come there from Moscow or the German lands. The others, bringing only sable, ermine and such-like, exchange their goods only for coats, shirts, hats, knives, spoons, needles, thread, choppers, looking-glasses and the like, for coins are not in use in their countries.

When embassies are sent to Moscow from Lithuania or other lands near by, merchants usually travel with them and are free of the duties levied both at the frontier and within. In the same way, when the Muscovites send an embassy their merchants travel with it, so that often eight hundred, a thousand, twelve hundred horses arrive in one mission.

The chief goods carried to Moscow are silver, woollen cloth, articles of silk or gold or silver, pearls, jewels, gold thread, and often occasional things of right poor quality which they exchange at high profit. Often some article is asked for which they do not have with them; the first to bring it makes much profit. As soon as other merchants learn of this they forward large quantities which then fall sharply in price, so that a trader may often buy back his own wares and make a handsome profit. The goods taken out of Moscow, especially to Germany, are furs and wax. To Lithuania and Turkey they send leather, skins, coarse furs and also fine ones. Thither too they send great white teeth, called fish teeth, which come from a beast living in the sea which they call *morsh* (walrus). From these they make fine hafts for weapons and knives. To Tartary they send saddles, bridles, coats and leather; no weapons or iron may be sent there. What they dispatch to the north and east has been told above of Kholopigorod. Such goods are also taken to Moscow at all seasons.

They are cunning and deceitful in their trade, making bold to offer their wares at three times their value and to take the seller's at less than half their worth; this takes place with much talk. As some have already written, they will often delay a month or two: he who can outlast the other has the best of the bargain. I bought fourteen *zimmer* (each of forty pieces) of sable, offered at eighteen hundred Hungarian gulden. I bid six hundred and the dealer let me ride away, thinking to outdo me. Later I sent the six hundred gulden to Moscow from Mozhaisk; the man gave me seven zimmer of the sables for three hundred gulden and a few ducats.

A merchant from Krakow brought in two hundred hundredweight of copper. The Prince was a bidder but kept him so long that he paid the customs dues and went back with his copper. When he had travelled a few leagues men were sent in pursuit to seize the goods as though he had circumvented the customs. He lodged complaint of this and the councillors offered to attend to the matter and, if he asked some favour, to grant it him. He was wily and knew that the Prince could not bear the shame of letting such goods out of the country, as though there were none rich enough to pay for them and as if the bargaining had been a mere pretence. The merchant sued only for justice, not for favour. Perceiving him so firm of purpose and understanding that he had marked their cunning, they paid him for his copper. Although they

Travel in winter. Single-horse sledges with 'duga'—harness as still used today; and skiers

will boldly ask a foreigner ten or twenty times the proper price they themselves will often make a bad bargain, paying much for what is inferior.

If they light upon a point favourable to themselves when they are dealing with others they clutch at it to their own advantage, and anything they say or promise is turned to their own favour, however they have pledged themselves, for they swear oaths only with the purpose of deceiving. I asked one of my attachés to help me make a purchase; he made me walk a long way and then ordered his own goods to be put before me. And the merchants ran up and begged him to help them sell their goods to me. Thus do these middlemen take from both sides when they promise their help.

Not far from the castle is a large walled house called the Lords' House. Here dwell the merchants, and often their goods are cheaper than in German lands. But this comes from their barter system.

Of every rouble's value of goods taken in or out, a duty of seven dengen falls to the Grand-duke—save for wax, taxed by weight at the rate of four dengen the *pud*, which is their weight.

Usury is common although recognized as one of the five chiefer sins. The churches are more lenient, taking but a tithe.

But in Kiev they have the right of claiming the property of any foreign merchant dying there, and it falls to the lord. The property carried by any merchant from Kiev who dies in Tatar or Turkish lands is also forfeit to the lord of that land. There is a hill there and when the merchants cross it, as they must, and the cart breaks down and can go no farther, the goods upon the cart fall to the lord.

The places are usually reached (in the Perm territory) upon *nartyn*, or snow-shoes. It is a piece of wood shaped like a board and a handsbreadth wide; it is about two long ells in length and turned up a little in front; in the middle the sides are turned up and between these rims are holes for binding the feet to it. When the snow grows hard a man may cover a great distance in a day. He holds a very short pike in his hand with which he may guide and assist himself when the way goes downhill or leads to a sharp drop. In these parts they travel much upon these nartyn. It is said also that they have great dogs drawing sledges.

VI
RELIGION

'The Russians have hitherto remained steadfastly true to their first creed, that of Greek Orthodoxy.'

The Russians have hitherto remained steadfastly true to their first creed, that of Greek Orthodoxy. All services are held in their language. They have no sermons; general confession and the reading of the Gospels take place in public near the altar. The Metropolitan General, as they call the head of their Church, previously had his seat in Kiev, then Vladimir; now it is in Moscow. Formerly there was a custom of making a circuit in Lithuania every seventh year, which took much money out of the country. Grand-duke Vitold would not allow this; he summoned his bishops and selected from among them a metropolitan to dwell in Minsk and now in Vilna, the capital. And although the Lithuanians and the capital of Vilna are of the Roman obedience, yet there are many more Russian than Roman churches there. The two Metropolitans of Moscow and Lithuania are answerable to the Patriarch in Constantinople.

In their chronicles the Russians are proud to relate how St Andrew the Apostle came from Greece up the River Dnieper and on to the hill where Kiev now stands, and how he blessed and baptized their country, setting up a cross and foretelling that many Christian churches would arise there.

Of old the metropolitans and the archbishops too were elected by the conclave of archbishops, bishops, abbots and priors of monasteries. In their convents and isolated hermitages they strove to find a better life and chose Andrew as their patron. When I was sent to Russia by Emperor Maximilian for the first time there was a metropolitan called Bartolomeus, who was counted a saint. When the Grand-duke broke the oath he had sworn, followed by this metropolitan, to Duke Shemyachich and made the latter prisoner, the archbishop addressed the prince on this and other matters, saying: 'Since you take all power unto yourself I cannot continue in my office.' He handed him his staff, which they call posokh, and surrendered his post. Quickly the Grand-duke grasped and annexed both the staff and the office. He had Bartholomew struck in irons and sent to the White Sea. They say he was kept prisoner there some while before he was set free, when he spent the rest of his life in a convent as a common monk.

After him one called Daniel was made metropolitan by the Grand-duke's influence; he was some thirty years of age and had a red face. So that this should not be seen by the multitude, who might conclude that he more often lay in debauch than prayer and fast, he had himself smoked with sulphur to pale him when he came to church to take service, using special appliances for the purpose.

Within the Muscovite territory are two archbishops, at Matigory near Novgorod and at Rostov. There are bishops at Tver, Ryazan, Smolensk, Perm, Susdal, Kolomna, Czernigov and Sarai, all under the Metropolitan. They have certain incomes from villages and dairy farms, called manor farms in some parts, as well as other dues. They have no castles or towns or other sign of station in the outer world. They renounce the eating of flesh for ever. I have only spoken to two abbots living in this district. But there are many priors, always appointed at the will of the Prince. How the priors were appointed previously may be gathered from an account by Warlam, prior of the monastery at Kutais in 7034 (1525). From it I have taken only a few of the main items. First the brethren petition the Grand-duke to appoint a worthy prior who can teach them the divine laws. When nominated he must, before his appointment is confirmed by the Prince, swear and affirm in writing that he will lead a good and holy life in the monastery according to the rules of the holy fathers, maintain all services according to custom and with the assent of the senior brethren, promoting a worthy man to each office, further faithfully the interests of the monastery, consult with three or four of the senior brethren about day-to-day affairs and carry their recommendations before the assembly of the brethren, concluding and executing all according to their counsel.

Nor is he to enjoy better food in private but always to eat at the common board and content himself with the common victuals of the other brethren. He is faithfully to collect all dues and income and deposit them in the convent's treasury. He must pledge himself to all this even if subjected to heavy penalty by the Grand-duke and displaced from his office. The elder brethren must also swear their loyalty to the prior in all this and promise faithful and constant obedience.

Priests are consecrated from among those who have served a certain term as church deacons. None is consecrated unless he have a lawful wife, and it commonly happens that such persons hold their nuptials before induction. But if the woman that the deacon wishes to take is not of good repute the consecration is refused and he is wedded to one who has a good name. When a priest's wife dies he becomes free of all ecclesiastical commitments and may do what he will, marrying again or taking up whatever craft or occupation that he will. If he wishes to remain one of the fathers and keeps himself chaste he may take part in services like other servants of the church and even enter the sanctuary. Previously it was the custom that, provided they remained chaste, priests could carry out their duties as before after becoming widowers. But now none such is allowed to hold mass or other services unless he betake himself to a monastery and conduct himself according to its rules and ordinances.

No priest may exercise his office by holding mass, baptizing and the like without the presence of his deacon. No priest may recite his obligatory prayers without a sacred image. The same applies to laymen with the prayers they have undertaken.

Priests are supreme within the church and he who should act or behave offensively towards the faith or his priestly office, whatever it may be, must pass before the judgment of the ecclesiastical court. But where one of them is accused of theft, drunkenness or other earthly misdemeanour he shall be punished by the public court. I and many others have seen how drunken priests in Moscow were beaten with scourges as they lay in the gutter. Their only complaint was that they should be beaten by a commoner, not a boyar. A few years ago the Grand-duke's governor caused a priest accused of theft to be hanged, and the Metropolitan lodged complaint with the Grand-duke. The governor was summoned and spoken to about it; he replied that, following the ancient custom of the country, he had hanged a thief and not a priest. He went unpunished.

It is to the public court that a priest makes petition against a layman, since the common court is competent in all cases of grievance or offence. And if it is found that the priest was the cause of the trouble or has treated the layman unjustly, then he is punished by the public judge.

Priests and churchmen are usually supported from church funds; they are allotted houses, fields and the like such as their neighbours have and gain their subsistence from them or cause their servants to do so. Their stipends are but small and in some places money is lent to the church at interest of ten to the hundred; from this the priests are provided for in order that they shall not need support from their own flock. Some of them are supported by the princes. But truly, few of them possess rents and revenues.

Tithes. When he was baptized Vladimir (St Vladimir), with the approval of the Metropolitan, ordered the setting aside of the tenth part of all things for the benefit of poor orphans, the sick, the aged, foreigners, prisoners, the burial of paupers, and also to assist those with large families and no food and those who had lost their property through fire: in brief, to help and comfort therewith all the poor, all needy convents and churches, all the faithful.

Nobody will give a living to any but a priest. There is but one altar in each church, and no more than one mass or service is held on one day in any church. Thus it is rare to find a church without an incumbent, and he has the obligation of celebrating mass on three days in the week. The priests dress like laymen but for a little coif with which they cover their tonsure, wearing over it a wide hat or else a long grey hat of otter's fur; each carries a staff upon which to rest, called posokh.

As already written, monasteries are ruled by abbots and priors, called *igumen* and *archimandrites*. They have strict and severe rules but moderate them to their comfort. They are allowed no pleasures; if one of them were found to have a lute he could not escape punishment. They must abjure the eating of flesh for ever. They must do obedience not only to the Grand-duke but to any boyar sent out by him. When I landed after journeying upon the Volga we came to the convent of St Elias, and my pristav requested something from the prior. When he refused, the pristav threatened him with the scourge and the monk very soon obeyed. Many leave the convents to go into the forests as hermits, living there pitifully. Alone in a cabin one of them or a pair live on the fruit of the trees and the roots in the ground. They are called *stolpniki. Stolp* is their word for a pillar; such huts stand commonly upon a pillar or stake.

When the metropolitans, archbishops or bishops have important guests on days when meat may be eaten—although they themselves have abjured it for ever—they are allowed the liberty of offering meat to their guests. But abbots and priors are not.

On two days of the feast of the Assumption I saw in Moscow a couple of the metropolitans mentioned conducting the service wearing their vestments. Their hoods do not swell as high as the ordinary kalpaks and are trimmed below with some two fingers of ermine, above which are set miniatures of the saints. The colour was red, if I remember aright. The other archbishops and bishops and the abbots have round black hats, but the Archbishop of Novgorod has a white hat or mitre similar to what our bishops wear. The vestments of the archbishops and bishops I did not see.

The daily costume of the bishops is very like that of the monks, save that it is sometimes of silk and that the cloak is, surprisingly, black. Over the heart are white strips signifying that streams of instruction, faith and good example flow from their hearts and mouths. They all carry crosiers to help them on their way or lean upon, the top of them being shaped like a cross; they are called posokh. The Archbishop of Novgorod wears a white cloak. Only devotion is usually expected of the archbishops; they have their officials to deal with matters of business.

They include in their calendar one or two popes whom they regard as holy but who, since the cleavage of the Churches, are disliked and decried as though they had renounced the teaching and laws of the apostles and the sacred fathers' councils. They hold them and us Catholics to be heterodox schismatics and hate us more than the Tatars. For they say that it was resolved at the seventh Oecumenical Council (787) that what had already been determined and concluded should remain unchanged for ever, and that no one should convoke or attend any Council from then onward under pain of ban and damnation. In the time of Pope Eugene a Russian metropolitan attended the Council and the two Churches reached an understanding (1439); when he returned home he was imprisoned and deposed, his property being seized. But he escaped.

This is how they baptize. As soon as the child is born they send for the priest, who stands on the threshold of the mother's room, says one or two of the set prayers and names the child. Usually on the fourteenth day thereafter, unless the child is sickly, it is taken to church and baptized, being plunged thrice into the water. Without this it would not be held baptized. It is then anointed with the chrism sanctified in Holy Week, then rubbed with what they call myrrh. The baptismal water is blessed especially for each child, and after the baptism it is poured forth at the church door. Children are baptized in church at any time unless they live too far away or might take harm from the cold. Lukewarm water is used only for those who are sick. Godparents are chosen by the father and mother and every time they renounce the devil they spit upon the ground. The parson always cuts the child's hair, kneads it in wax and sets it aside in the church. They use no salt nor spittle and earth.

Of confession. Although confession is governed by rules it is to the common man something pertaining to princes, noblemen and important people. They make confession at Eastertide with full repentance and reverence. Confessor and penitent stand in the midst of the church, both looking towards a designated image. When confession is done and penance settled they bow before the image and sign themselves on head, bosom and both shoulders, touching themselves with the first three fingers together. And with much sighing they say aloud: 'Jesus Christ, Son of God, take pity on us.' And that is the entire prayer of the common man. Some are made to fast, others to say prayers—though few common people can say the paternoster—and for some sins they are made to wash. At Epiphany they take water from a flowing stream and keep it in consecration in the church throughout the year for the washing away of great sins. Sins committed on a Saturday are held less grievous and require a lesser penance. There are many slighter trespasses for which the church is forbidden them, but they may hear or see the service through the door of the sanctuary or the window that it usually has. He who has intercourse with his wife before midnight on Twelfth Night may wash and go to church, but not if it was after midnight.

The taking of the Sacrament. They receive the sacrament in both forms. When they desire to bless it they mix wine and bread together. Each communicant who presents himself receives a small loaf of bread, with one for the priest. These rolls have words impressed in the middle of the upper crust, and the square surrounding this portion is cut out with a special prayer and laid upon the paten: it is for the priest. From the remainder, destined for the communicants, he cuts a sector and lays it with the rest upon the paten. At the proper time he places all these pieces in the chalice and then adds the wine and water. When the time for partaking arrives the priest takes a small spoon, removes his own portion, and gives each communicant a piece with the spoon.

And provided he attends confession a man may communicate as often in the year as he will. But the usual time is at Easter. The sacrament is administered to children of seven years, for they hold them capable of sin at this age. If a child is too weakly to enjoy the sacrament, a drop from the chalice is put into his mouth. (The sacred host serving for communion is consecrated during mass.) For the sick, bread and wine are consecrated on Maundy Thursday and kept throughout the year. When need arises a small piece is taken out and softened in wine; lukewarm water is added and it is given to the sufferer. This medley of bread and wine before its transubstantiation is venerated when carried round before mass as though it were itself a sacrament.

Of Priestly Prayers, Sacred Images and Books of the Gospel. No monk or priest recites his daily office without a holy image before him, which he takes or touches with marked reverence. If he carries it across the street he holds it high in the air and all who pass by sign themselves and bow in reverence. They put the Gospels in places of honour as sacred objects. They make use of them only after crossing themselves and bowing with bared head, and take them up with much reverence.

Feast Days. After church, important or wealthy people celebrate feast days by good eating and drinking and more ceremonious dress. Poor people go to work as on other days, saying: 'Feasting and idling are for the lords.' Town-dwellers and artisans go to church and then work as at other times, holding work better than drinking, gaming or the like, and wasting their substance. Drinking mead and beer is forbidden to the common folk save at certain times of the year, at Christmas, Shrovetide, Easter, Whitsun and a few other fixed seasons. They celebrate on these occasions more on account of the drink than from reverence. The first time I asked to be taken to church in the castle, on the feast of the Assumption, I saw many poor peasants at work in the grounds. They celebrate Holy Trinity on the Monday of Whitsuntide, and All Saints on the Sunday after Pentecost. Corpus Christi they do not observe. When they take an oath they kiss the cross. They abuse each other much as do the Hungarians: 'May the dogs pollute your mother.'

Of Purgatory or Limbo. They think naught of purgatory, saying that the soul of every mortal has a place marked out for it according to his merits upon earth, a bright one with tender angels for the blessed and, for those who have earned no grace, a gloomy one with angels who cause them terror and afflict them in other ways. In these places they await the Last Judgment. Those in the light with the good angels are comforted by the grace of God and pray daily for the Day of Judgment; the others the reverse, saying that the soul cannot suffer without the body and is not responsible for it, and that if both have sinned together it would be unjust to torment the one and leave the other in peace. Through their prayers and offerings for the souls of the departed they think to provide them with gentler harbourage and lessened affliction as they await the Doomsday.

None besprinkles himself with holy water, which is acceptable only from a priest. They do not consecrate ground for burials, saying that the earth does not sanctify the body but the body the earth.

Of Saints. They revere St Nicholas, who lies at Bari in the kingdom of Naples, above all others and tell of his many wondrous deeds, one of which is said to have taken place but a few years ago. An illustrious Muscovite soldier called Michael Kisaletski had routed a notable Tatar, and when Michael could not catch the Tatar up he cried aloud to St Nicholas: 'Help me to catch the Tatar!' The Tatar heard this and spoke: 'Nicholas, if he catches me with your help it will be no miracle. But if you save me, who do not know you, then great will be your fame.' They tell how Michael's horse stood still and the Tatar escaped him. From then on this same Tatar sent Michael each year a quantity of honey to be given to the poor in honour of St Nicholas, with a portion for himself and a splendid coat of marten.

Fasts. The fasts before Easter they call the great fasts and observe them seven weeks long. In the first of them they may partake of a dish made from milk, called *syrna* and akin to cheese. In all the other weeks they eat no fish either (save for those who make a journey). At this season there are some who eat on Saturdays and Sundays, abstaining from all food on other days, and others who eat only on Sunday, Tuesday, Thursday and Saturday, fasting on the other days. There are also those who eat no more than a piece of bread on Monday, Thursday and Saturday. The later fasts are less strictly observed; they begin to fast on the Monday of Trinity week, on which they celebrate All Saints, and continue until St Peter's and St Paul's Day, which is called St Peter's fast. Then comes the fast of Our Lady, lasting from the first day of August until the Assumption. And if St Peter's and St Paul's or Our Lady's should fall upon a Wednesday or Friday they fast then just the same.

In Advent they fast six whole weeks, the fast of St Philip, for by their calendar St Philip's Day falls upon the 14th of November. On the other hand they fast on none of the eves save for that of the martyrdom of St John, whose feast they hold upon the 29th of August. If some notable saint's day falls within the fasts, such as St Matthew's or the Annunciation, they will eat fish upon this day. The fasting of the monks is much more strict, who may comfort themselves only with a drink, that is common water thickened with gruel or dough.[1] At these times priests are forbidden to drink mead and beer, even though their rules permit it. On Saturday they eat meat, renouncing it in return on Wednesday.

The Teachers that they follow. These are Basilius (Vassili the Great), St Gregory, St John Chrysostumus—called also 'of the golden mouth' —and Zlatoust. They have no preachers, deeming it sufficient to hold their service in the common language which they hear and understand daily from the priests in the church. They also hold that many errors and heresies have arisen from sermons. Public confessions and the feast and fast days of the coming week are announced by the priests on Saturday. And whatever the Grand-duke believes or thinks right is normally accepted by them.

At this time we were told privily that the Patriarch in Constantinople had dispatched, at the wish of the Grand-duke, a monk named Maximilian to overlook all books, laws and ordinances affecting the faith, set them in good order and make them of clear intelligence. And he had done this, finding many grievous errors, and laid all before the Grand-duke, whom he held to be truly a heretic following neither the Roman nor the Greek usage. And although honourably received by the Prince he disappeared soon after, having been drowned as many of them thought. Three years before our arrival Marcus, a Greek merchant from Kaffa, had also been in Moscow and spoken in the same vein. He was seized, despite the patient and vigorous intervention of the Turkish ambassador, and taken away. (. . .)

Their churchmen show great zeal in bringing the multitude to the Christian faith. By dint of their teaching, holy life and spreading of the word of God the monks and hermits have brought many heresies within the fold of Christianity and continue to do so. At the same time they have gone into the desert and the infidel regions towards the south and east, reaching them with no little danger, hunger and toil and without thought of worldly recompense, striving only to win souls for the Lord and bring them to the true faith. Often they have affirmed the Christian teaching by the manner of their death.

There is a renowned convent of the Holy Trinity twelve leagues westward from Moscow where St Sergius lies buried and, they say, still works many wonders. There is a great concourse of people there each year; the Grand-duke has often gone and regaled all those within the convent. They say there is a pot or pan of copper in which the

[1] Kvass?

meat and usually the herbs too are cooked. Few or many may arrive: they are fed from this vessel, and always enough remains for the nourishment of the servitors. Nothing goes astray and there is never any surplus.

As I have already written, the Muscovites vaunt themselves as the true Christians and condemn us as having forsaken the original Church and its ancient holy principles. Thus when, at or even against the wish of his lord, a Catholic comes to them alleging a religious motive they do not intend to deliver him up again even if he were sent by his master. (. . .)

When the Prince bids the Metropolitan to his table and neither of his brothers is there he gives him the place of honour. But when a funeral service is held and the Metropolitan and bishops are invited he serves them himself to begin with. Then he orders one of his brothers or some other prince to act in his stead until the end of the meal.

So that I might witness their worship I succeeded in gaining admission to the chief of their churches on each of the two Assumptions when I was there. The church was bestrewn with the branches of trees, and by no means small ones, right up to the entrance to the choir. In the midst of it was a platform raised upon two steps and here stood the Metropolitan in his ceremonial robes, wearing his little cap and carrying the staff or posokh, upon which he leaned. Their chasubles are bell-shaped; they roll them up at the arm so that they may use their hands. His deacons and others stood by him and he made his prayers upon the platform; a deacon held a roll before him from which he drew forth the sheets of parchment himself. The choir sang during this time.

The Grand-duke stood by the door through which he enters the church, his back against the wall and leaning upon his staff. His hat and kalpak were borne by one standing before him who had pulled down his sleeves and wrapped them round his fingers so that the hand he had within the hat looked like a block of wood. His councillors stood by the columns of the church, as I was doing. After the singing and prayers the Metropolitan went down from the platform to the choir in the middle of the church, his long robe causing him to lift his feet high over the branches. They took their stations in the choir and then the priests, deacons and Metropolitan made a progress down through the narrow door to the right, turning then to the left and coming back into the midst of the church up through the larger doorway, the very opposite of our processions. One of the deacons bore upon his head the paten on which lay the bread, covered with a small cloth, to be used for the sacrament, and another carried the chalice already filled with wine.

Several holy portraits were carried forward upon their cloths, such as those of St Peter, St Nicholas, the archangels. The priests wore richly ornamented vestments. The people showed much reverence before the images, bread and wine, sighing, weeping and striking their brows upon the ground. There was no more room in the sanctuary and this prevented me from learning if they were really celebrating communion. One and all cried out aloud: 'Lord have mercy upon us, Lord have mercy upon us!' Then they began high mass, performing the whole service in their own tongue, with much *Kyrie eleison* and *Christe eleison* but only in their own language, and sang *Gospodin pomilui.* The Epistle and the Gospel were read loudly and clearly from a high desk outside the choir. When the priest had eaten his portion and the communicants were to partake, the deacon bearing the chalice of consecrated wine stepped into the central doorway of the choir and cried: 'Here is the body of Our Lord!' and then moved backwards to the altar close by the door of the choir.

Portrait of the author in old age

APPENDIX

THE BACKGROUND TO HERBERSTEIN'S MISSION

The Eastern Slavonic peoples set up the first state of importance around Kiev in the ninth century, accepting the Christianity of Constantinople. The Grand-duchy of Kiev was perpetually on the defensive against the pressure of Turkish tribes from the east such as the Pechenegs and the Kumans (Polovtsi). In 1240 it succumbed to the onslaught of the Mongols, who also conquered Budapest and Gran (Esztergom) and Cracow. The Russians' political centre of gravity entrenched itself in the forests north of the steppe, where a number of principalities took shape; in 1299 the Metropolitan of 'Kiev and all Russia' moved his seat from Kiev to Vladimir, between Moscow and Nizhniy Novgorod.

The Russian principalities were tributary to the Golden Horde, which had its capital in Sarai on the lower Volga. Advancing from the west the principality of Lithuania swallowed up White Russia including Smolensk in about 1300, and the Ukraine including Kiev in 1320. Waves of Turkish peoples were gradually absorbing their Mongolian overlords and forming independent Tatar khanates, such as those of the Crimea and of Kazan on the middle Volga. With their forays, even these constituted a permanent threat to the Russian Grand-duchies. For purposes of defence these territories were gradually grouped under the principality of Moscow, and the Russian boundary to the east and south was later populated by a feudal tenantry of Cossacks, and hence a military frontier, down to the nineteenth century.

Emergence of Moscow

The rising Grand-duchy of Moscow shook off its vassalage to the waning Golden Horde and the Tatars and began to strengthen its relations with the south—Byzantium and the Rumanian Grand-duchies of Moldavia and Wallachia, and with the west—Lithuania, united in 1386 with Poland under Ladislas Jagellon, and Hungary. The Council of Ferrara and Florence of 1438–9 was attended not only by the Byzantine Emperor John Paleologue VIII and the pro-union Archbishop of Nicea Bessarion, appointed Roman Cardinal in 1439, but by a strong Russian delegation headed by Isidore, Metropolitan of Moscow. A member of the delegation, presumably a secular official attached to the Bishop of Susdal, drew up an interesting report upon this journey. The result of the attempted union of churches, which collapsed later in Byzantium, was regarded by the Russians as a betrayal of orthodoxy and decided them to take their own course in religion also.

Impact of the Turks

The Osmanli were the last of the Turkish peoples to thrust west and south; they combined, in what might be called the last convulsion of the Migration of Nations, the impetuosity of youth with the enthusiasm of recent converts to the Muslim faith. In 1453 came the fall of the last of the Byzantine emperors, the Paleologue Constantine XI, who had begun his reign in 1448 at the siege of Constantinople. Territorially the Ottomans inherited the Byzantine succession, the sultans of Istanbul adding to their titles that of Kaisar-i-Rum or Emperor of Rome. In addition Sultan Mehmet II (Fatim the Conqueror, 1451–1481) subdued in 1460 the joint rule of the Paleologues in the Peloponnesus, the so-called despotism of Morea, that of the Comnenes in northern Asia Minor in 1462 (the empire of Trebizond) and also all Serbia and Bosnia in 1458 and 1463. After the principalities of Moldavia and Wallachia, together with Albania, had been laid under tribute the threat of the Ottoman Empire soon turned towards Hungary, Austria and Bohemia.

The Third Rome

The last tyrant (*despotes*) of Morea, Thomas, fled with his children to Rome in 1460. He brought with him as a valuable relic the head of the apostle Andrew from Patras; this was handed over by the Vatican to the Greek Church in 1964. After Thomas's death in 1465 his daughter Zoe-Sofia, who lived in Rome under the protection of Cardinal Bessarion and whose trousseau was provided by the Pope, married the Grand-duke of Moscow Ivan III (1462–1505). But the hopes fixed by Pope Sixtus IV upon the realization in Russia of the principles of the Union of Florence were not fulfilled. In Sofia the Grand-duke of Moscow had married a niece of the last East Roman Emperor. This and the steady rise of Moscow, combined with the preservation of pure orthodoxy, led on to Russia's special sense of vocation as the product of New Zion and the Third Roman Empire.

It was then that the monk Philotheos (Filofei) was to write to Vassili III (1505–33), with whom Herberstein negotiated in Moscow in 1517 and 1527: 'All Christian realms have been transformed together into your single Empire. Two Romes have indeed fallen but the third stands, and there will be no fourth.' It was the boyar (prince) Andrew Kurbski, who had fled to Poland before Ivan IV (1533–84) who was to coin the term 'Holy Russia' in his exile. The guardianship of orthodoxy was transferred from Byzantium to Russia, and together with the emblem of the double-headed eagle went something of the Byzantine political role of defence against the east and south, then represented by the Tatars and the Osmanli.

The Jagellonic Empire

From the Balkans and the lower Danube the Ottomans now made their thrust against the eastern portions of central Europe. The latinized occident, with its diverse policies, had been dawdling all too long over the concentration of its defences. The papal plans for a Crusade met with a feeble response. The imminent alliance of Hungary with Austria came to grief because of the personal antipathy between the Emperor Frederick III (1440–93) and Matthew Corvinus, King of Hungary (1458–90). After his death the Hungarian nobility, now opposed to the dominion of the Hunyadis, elected the Jagellon Ladislas II (1490–1516), who had been King of Bohemia since 1471.

With Poland—comprising also Lithuania, White Russia and the Ukraine—Bohemia and Hungary this Jagellonic coalition extending from the Baltic to the Danube could have have been an obstacle to the Ottomans. Such an alliance would at the same time have completely stifled the Habsburgs in Austria, much as the Luxemburg dynasty, operating from Bohemia, had once forced the Habsburgs into the background for a whole century.

Treaty between Frederick III and Ivan III

In spite of the growing menace of the Turks the Habsburgs had been seeking since 1485 to obstruct this Jagellonic league and its threat to the Austrian dynasty, notably by means of an alliance with the Grand Duchy of Moscow which sought to reclaim White Russia and the Ukraine from Poland-cum-Lithuania as former Russian territories. Through his envoy Nikolaus von Popplau, sent to Moscow in 1488, Emperor Frederick III offered Ivan III both an anti-Polish alliance and the hand of his nephew, Margrave Albert of Baden, for one of Ivan's daughters.

The Russian counter-mission under Georg (Yury) Trachaniotes, the 'little Greek', was ceremoniously received by Frederick III and Maximilian in 1489, for many Byzantines were refugees in Moscow. Trachaniotes and the Austrian ambassador Jörg von Thurn travelled to Moscow in 1490, where a treaty was signed which was to be valid during the lifetime of Ivan III and Maximilian. The latter sued personally for the hand of one of Ivan's daughters. The Russian counter-mission reached Maximilian in Nuremberg in March 1491, and in the following November Thurn handed over Maximilian's treaty document in Moscow.

An anti-Turkish Alliance proposed

Meanwhile Ladislas, the Jagellonian King of Bohemia, had been elected to the throne of Hungary after the death of Matthew Corvinus. In the treaty of Bratislava (1492), however, it had been agreed with the consent of the Hungarian Diet that Maximilian should become King of Hungary if Ladislas died without male issue. In 1492 Maximilian drew the attention of the next Russian mission to the Turkish threat and the possibility of a grand alliance between Austria, Bohemia, Poland, Lithuania and Russia against the Ottomans.

Soon after his accession to the throne Vassili III (1505–53) sent a letter to Maximilian seeking the renewal of the alliance of 1490–1: the two potentates were to assist each other in regaining their 'hereditary' lands, Hungary and White Russia. Maximilian evaded it. After the death of Casimir IV of Poland (1445–92), married to the ambitious Habsburg Elizabeth—daughter of Albert II and sister of Ladislas Posthumus—his sons Jan Olbracht (1492–1501), Alexander I (1501–1506) and finally Sigismund I (1506–48) became Kings in succession.

With his marriage to Barbara Zapolya Sigismund I set himself up as the champion of the anti-Habsburg party in Hungary, and the observance of the treaty of Bratislava was jeopardized. In 1514 Maximilian sent the lord of Pettau, Georg Schnitzenpaumer, to Moscow to negotiate with Vassili III and his council of boyars a fresh treaty in which Vassili is described as Emperor of Russia. In March of the same year Schnitzenpaumer came back with a Russian mission led by the Greek Dmitri Laskirev (to whom a Russian official, Elizar Zhukhov, had been attached) to Maximilian, who altered the treaty and had it taken to Moscow in December 1514 by the envoys Dr Jacob Osler and Moritz Burgstaller.

An Earlier Congress of Vienna

Sigismund of Poland was now obliged to alter course. With Ladislas II of Bohemia and Hungary as an intermediary, a compromise was worked out by Maximilian's councillor Crispinian and the Polish Deputy Chancellor Szydlowiecki and accepted at the Princes' Congress in Vienna in 1515. Maximilian renounced his support of the Teutonic Order against Poland and recognized the provisions of the Peace of Thorn, 1467—all the more readily because the Electors of Saxony and Brandenburg rejected any collective measures against Poland. Maximilian also restricted the obligations of his alliance with Vassili III.

Sigismund I and the Jagellons gave up their great-power schemes. Maximilian adopted the nine-year old Ludwig, son of Ladislas of Bohemia and Hungary, and gave him the hand of his granddaughter Maria, whilst Ludwig's sister, the thirteen-year-old Anna, was destined for Archduke Ferdinand. But these contracts of marriage and inheritance in no way conveyed sovereignty over the dominions concerned. For this the assent of the Diet was required, and it is common knowledge that it was given fully in the case of the Bohemian succession in 1526 only after long negotiations, and in Hungary, on account of the adverse vote of John Zapolya, only with reservations.

In the war with Poland the Russians had captured Smolensk and suffered a defeat at Orsha; now they were besieging Vitebsk and Polotsk. To the Russian mission (Alexei Zabolocki and Diak Shtshekin) which exhorted him upon his obligations at the end of March 1515 Maximilian offered only his intervention between Vassili and Sigismund I. By dispatching the couriers Balthasar Eder and then Georg Raumschüssel, who was supported by the Russian envoy Afanasi Kuritsyn, Maximilian sought to calm things down. But later, and together with another of Vassili III's envoys, he sent to Moscow for the first time Sigmund von Herberstein.

Herberstein's Mission to Poland

This background to Herberstein's missions may serve to put his *Moscovia* into historical perspective; further details may be found in Hans Uebersberger's account *Austria and Russia since the end of the*

15th century, vol. i, 1488–1605, published in 1906. Herberstein went to see King Sigismund in Vilna; he was able to carry out his first commission with success and given Bona Sforza as his second wife by Maximilian. As representative of the allies of Vassili III Herberstein interested himself in the Russians fallen into Polish captivity at Orsha, visiting their leader Ivan Cheladin in prison. His travelling companion, the Russian envoy Zagraiskoi, was taken by the Poles to the frontier under strict guard and by a devious route. But Vassili and his Boyar Council demanded terms for their intervention in the cause of peace which were unacceptable to the Polish monarch, so that Herberstein's first mission was without political result.

In November 1517 he left Moscow in the company of a Russian deputation (Vladimir Semionov Plemiannikov and the interpreter Istoma Malyi) charged with summoning Maximilian finally to the observance of his obligations as ally. From Innsbruck the deputation travelled back to Moscow with new envoys from Maximilian, Francesco da Collo from Conegliano and Antonio de' Conti from Padua, but even the Italian diplomats could achieve nothing in Moscow. In 1522, however, a five-year armistice between Poland and Moscow, on a *status quo* basis, was concluded without the intervention of Austria, although the prisoners on both sides, about whom the Russians were especially concerned, were not released.

Maximilian dead

Maximilian's death, the start of the Reformation, Austria's struggle with France and the difficulties arising from the accession of Ferdinand in the former country caused Vassili III to send an embassy to Emperor Charles V in Madrid. He referred it, however, to Ferdinand, adding to it his own envoy, Count Leonhard Nogarola. The latter and Herberstein, now on his second errand to Moscow, were received by Vassili on 1 May 1526. In 1525 Dmitri Gerasimov, who had assisted Maximus the Greek in his translation of the Psalms and knew both Latin and German, had been sent by Grand-duke Vassili to Pope Clement VII in Rome, and the Pope sent back to Moscow the Bishop of Scara as his nuncio.

On 5 November 1526, in the presence of Herberstein, Nogarola and the nuncio, the armistice treaty between Poland and Moscow was solemnly affirmed by Vassili III and the ambassador of Sigismund I in the persons of the Paladin of Polotsk and Marshal Bogus Bogotinovitz, two members of the Lithuanian nobility. The five-year treaty seems very favourable to Grand-duke Vassili; the nomination of the three mediators desired by these noblemen and by the ambassadors of Poland-Lithuania, was not accepted by the Russians, who insisted that the armistice was a bilateral instrument. Presumably accompanied by the Russian envoys Liapun Osinin and Andrei Volosati, Herberstein and Nogarola returned via Cracow. The Bishop of Scara was escorted by the envoys Yeremi Trusov and Sharap Lodygin, whom the Pope was to assist in recruiting Italian artists and craftsmen for the Grand-duke.

The Holy League

Whilst the representatives of Spain and Burgundy, Austria and the Pope, were negotiating the Russo-Polish armistice in Moscow an alliance of the whole of western Europe—France, Pope Clement VII, Venice and Milan—had been concluded on 22 May 1526 in the form of the Holy League of Cognac against the dominance of the Habsburg confederacy of Spain, Burgundy, Austria and states loyal to the Emperor. Louis II of Hungary was killed in the battle of Mohacs on 29 August 1526: the gap in the succession that Frederick III had hoped for had arrived. In Bohemia Ferdinand triumphed over the other claimants—above all the Wittelsbach candidates—and was unanimously elected king.

In Hungary a portion of the nobility elected Johann Zapolyas to the throne, and this was supported by Bavaria, Poland and the Ottomans, but there was a long struggle for the crown ending in the trisection of Hungary for a hundred and forty years. Western and northern Hungary remained under Habsburg dominion, central Hungary became a Turkish pashalic—the Turks besieging Vienna for the first time in 1529 and being repulsed at Güns ten years later—and Transylvania, initially under the Zapolyas, became an autonomous principality which was long a vassal of the Ottoman Empire. It was liberated after the second siege of Vienna in 1683 and, like central Hungary, reinserted into the system governed by the crown of St Stephen.

Poland supplanted

In contrast to the far-flung Jagellonian commonwealth stretching southward from Lithuania and Poland to Bohemia and Hungary, the Habsburgs of Austria had at last been able to achieve their trinity of Austrian, Bohemian and Hungarian territories from components which were geographically and militarily compatible. It had not been merely the dynasty's shrewd policy regarding marriage and inheritance